THE SERMON ON THE MOUNT

See these other books by E. Wayne Stucki available at your favorite ebook retailer:

Ascendance

Liberty

Betrayal

Mars (Upcoming)

If you wish to learn more about upcoming books you can contact the author at ewaynestucki@gmail.com.

THE SERMON ON THE MOUNT

A Christlike Approach to Loving and Leading in the Latter Days

E. WAYNE STUCKI

Copyright 2024 by E. Wayne Stucki

All rights reserved, including the right to reproduce this book, or portions thereof, in any form. No part of this book may be used or reproduced in any manner whatsoever without written permission from the publisher, except in the case of brief quotations embodied in critical articles and reviews. The views expressed herein are the responsibility of the author and do not necessarily represent the position of the publisher. For information or permission, contact ewaynestucki@gmail.com.

This is a work of creative nonfiction. The events herein are portrayed to the best of the author's memory. While all the stories in this book are true, some names and identifying details may have been changed to protect the privacy of the people involved.

This work is not an official production of The Church of Jesus Christ of Latter-day Saints. The views that are expressed within this work are the sole responsibility of the author and do not necessarily reflect the position of The Church of Jesus Christ of Latter-day Saints or any other entity. All quotes by Latter-day Saint leaders are copyrighted by Intellectual Reserve, Inc.

Cover design by Jessica Warner

Interior print design and layout by Sydnee Hyer

Ebook design and layout by Sydnee Hyer

Published by Red Willow Publishing

Paperback 979-8-9884608-8-6
Ebook 979-8-9884608-9-3

CONTENTS

Author's Note	vii
Introduction	1
Blessed Are the Persecuted	9
Blessed Are the Peacemakers	29
Blessed Are the Pure in Heart	49
Blessed Are the Merciful	81
Blessed Are They Which Do Hunger and Thirst after Righteousness	105
Blessed Are the Meek	147
Blessed Are They That Mourn	169
Blessed Are the Poor in Spirit	191
Summary	223
About the Author	231

AUTHOR'S NOTE

The following is a discussion of the Sermon on the Mount. It is written from the perspective of the author, who is an active member of The Church of Jesus Christ of Latter-day Saints (the Mormons). Members of The Church of Jesus Christ of Latter-day Saints have been labeled as "non-Christians" by many other faiths. This work will demonstrate that we believe in Christ, though our specific theology may differ from traditional Christianity.

Because of this perspective, there are terms and references in this work that those not acquainted with our faith would not have a frame of reference. Efforts have been made through the writing to explain various terms which may not seem self-explanatory.

INTRODUCTION

With the development of civilization, leaders needed to be trained and prepared. Effective leaders produced greater harvests or generated successful hunts, which ensured the survival of the village, clan, or tribe. As part of their responsibilities, the village elders or council selected suitable successors whom their people would follow and then passed on to those leaders the necessary experience and wisdom.

As the villages, clans, and tribes developed into nations, the need for effective leaders became even more apparent. Defenses had to be prepared, food production had to increase, and laws had to be enforced for the safety and well-being of the nation's citizens. Although training attempted to meet the increasing need for leaders, it was spotty and inadequate by today's standards.

The creation of a merchant class expanded the field of people that required training. An even greater effort was directed toward improving the effectiveness of what a person could accomplish. If a merchant, ranch foreman, steward, corporate officer, or business manager was not able to motivate those under their direction, production ceased, profits suffered, and the organization failed.

During the twentieth century with two major wars, several lesser conflicts, and changes in technology, those who were or would be considered leaders expanded exponentially. To improve the training for those leaders, research was conducted, corporations were formed, and books outlining recognized leadership principles were published. In addition, seminars sponsored by all types of organizations supplemented this training with examples and experiences.

The Church of Jesus Christ of Latter-day Saints has been in the vanguard of efforts to train its lay leaders. During the first century of its existence, people were often called to positions they did not know how to fulfill and lead. They learned by experience and revelation (*personal receipt of inspiration and answers to prayer for direction and guidance*). Then, the Church developed a manual of instructions and an initial orientation for those called to the Lord's work. This manual acquainted the individual with their responsibilities. Auxiliary to the orientation, the Church created follow-up training meetings (both personally and as a group) to aid in the successful completion of the call.

With all these aids for leadership training available through either the Church or other sources, it is up to each individual person to learn the necessary principles and put them into practical use. In March 1835, the Lord told the Prophet Joseph Smith (*the founding leader of the Church beginning April 6, 1830, who is recognized by Church membership as a prophet such as in the times of Moses*),

> Wherefore, now let every man learn his duty, and to act in the office in which he is appointed, in all diligence.
>
> He that is slothful shall not be counted worthy to stand, and he that learns not his duty and shows himself not approved shall not be counted worthy to stand. (Doctrine and Covenants 107:99–100—*a book recognized as scripture by the Church. It is comprised of a series of revelations received*

mainly by the Prophet Joseph Smith during the formation and growth of the Church in the 1800s.)

The early Church leaders of the Restoration (*the contemporary time period when the Church that Jesus Christ established while he was ministering in Palestine is being restored to the earth*) did not have the opportunity to learn leadership principles through the methods which currently exist. Priesthood leadership meetings, manuals, seminars, camps, classes, and other books are new developments inspired by God to assist in the spread of the gospel and aid in the exaltation of God's children. Joseph Smith and others had to be taught from the scriptures or by direct revelation how to direct the affairs of the kingdom of God.

In the meridian of time (*the period of the mortal ministry of Christ and the time of the Apostles immediately after*), those who directed Christ's Church after his death and resurrection came from varied walks of life. Their training and experience had been directed toward fishing, carpentry, orchard management, or other ways of putting food on the table. With their call to serve as leaders in the Church, they had to learn new skills and techniques. To accomplish this feat, they had their share of scriptures but had the added blessing of being taught by the Savior himself.

Christ was born during a time when Israel had fallen away from God and had been conquered by the Romans. In spite of the harsh rule imposed by their conquerors for decades, the nation of Israel had not collectively chosen to repent and follow God. Their situation had remained in this state for years because the rulers of the Jews were more interested in maintaining their own power and influence than in obedience to the spirit of the commandments. The Sanhedrin and those placed in authority by the Romans strengthened their rule by using, misusing, and corrupting the beliefs and teachings of God, which were intended to save the people. Those who opposed Rome likewise desired power rather than righteousness and interpreted the prophecies regarding the expected Messiah to aid in their efforts. They taught that the expected Savior would raise armies to free Israel from its oppressors rather than conquer sin and death.

In the midst of apostasy (*in this case, Israel falling away from the truth*) and unrealistic expectations, the Savior began his ministry. His responsibility was to atone for the sins of mankind and restore purity to the commandments and ordinances of God. Christ also had to establish an organization that would continue his work after he was gone. To accomplish this purpose, Jesus selected and ordained those who would assist him. Then came the task to instruct, to buttress, and to train.

The first known priesthood leadership training session occurred during the Savior's second Galilean ministry. By this time, Christ had been baptized by John, cleansed the temple, taught multitudes of people, and performed several miracles. He had accomplished enough to gain a certain amount of notoriety. After being rejected by his friends and neighbors at Nazareth, the Savior selected twelve men from among his followers to be his Apostles. These men were Simon (better known as Peter), Andrew, James, John, Phillip, Bartholomew, Matthew, Thomas, James (son of Alphaeus), Simon, Judas, and Judas Iscariot (see Luke 6:13–16). With this selection and ordination complete, the Savior went up into the mountains near the Sea of Galilee. He wanted this time away from the crowds who sought him to prepare for his next task of training his Apostles. At the appropriate time, the Savior sent for those selected special witnesses (see Matthew 5:1), and their instruction began.

Several years later, after having completed his mortal ministry in Palestine, a resurrected Christ descended to the land Bountiful in the Americas, which is recorded in the Book of Mormon. The people who were gathered around the temple had survived the devastating natural catastrophes that accompanied the Savior's death. By enduring the whirlwinds, earthquakes, floods, volcanoes, and darkness, they now had the opportunity to touch the Redeemer's wounds and confirm the existence of their Savior. Just as he had in Palestine, Christ called leaders to administer his Church after he left. Again, he set about to perform the necessary training.

Because principles of leadership remain the same worldwide, the training given to those in Palestine and those in the land Bountiful was similar. In some instances, the wording used by Christ was identical. But because the presentation had to be tailored to different peoples and cultures and the fact the Savior had completed the Atonement, there were differences in wording and emphasis.

These two sermons—or different versions of the same sermon—constitute the first recorded priesthood leadership meeting. Even today, after many centuries, in different circumstances and forms, these same principles are taught to church leaders. Because of this, the Sermon on the Mount is a primer for church leadership.

In both America and Palestine, the Savior began training the leaders of his Church by introducing the categories or principles they would be taught. This order follows the concept of telling the listener what they are going to hear, teaching the idea, and summarizing what they heard. Modern research has learned that repetition in this manner increases retention. Thus, it is no surprise that the Master Teacher would use techniques to enhance his students learning. The eight areas Christ introduced have come to be known as the Beatitudes. They are as follows:

> Blessed are the poor in spirit
> Blessed are they that mourn

Blessed are the meek

Blessed are they who hunger and thirst after righteousness

Blessed are the merciful

Blessed are the pure in heart

Blessed are the peacemakers

Blessed are the persecuted

(refer to Matthew 5:3–10)

After reciting the topics to be discussed, Christ, using a literary device known as chiasmus, went on to explain in detail which aspects of these topics his leaders needed to know and practice. He began with the last topic given, that of being persecuted, and made his presentation. Then the Beatitude of being peacemakers was discussed. In this study, each Beatitude or leadership principle will be examined in the same order as they were originally presented by the Savior. Any difference between the Sermon given in Palestine and that presented in Bountiful will also be examined. Teachings by other prophets, modern or ancient, which supplement the concept, will be reviewed.

These topics will be examined within the framework of Christ's work to exalt God's children (see Moses 1:39 *contained in a book called the Pearl of Great Price*) for all his actions then, as they are now, were directed toward this goal. He said: "For God doth not walk in crooked paths, neither doth he turn to the right hand nor to the left, neither doth he vary from that which he hath said, therefore his paths are straight, and his course is one eternal round" (Doctrine and Covenants 3:2).

Each Beatitude has an associated blessing which complies with God's purpose of helping his children receive immortality and achieving eternal life. The poor in spirit and those who are persecuted receive the kingdom of heaven, a synonym for the celestial kingdom (*the realm where*

God and Christ dwell). The meek inherit the earth, which will become a celestial body and residence for Christ; the celestial kingdom for those of this planet. The pure in heart will see God, a reward for those who live celestial laws. Peacemakers are called children of God, and children will inherit all that their parents have. The other Beatitudes receive blessings which assist in living celestial laws on earth. Those who mourn are comforted. The merciful obtain mercy. They who hunger and thirst after righteousness are filled with the Holy Ghost. Those who desire the blessings associated with a particular Beatitude must be obedient to that Beatitude (see Doctrine and Covenants 130:20–21).

The premise of this work is that by understanding and living the concepts contained in the Sermon on the Mount, a leader becomes more God-like and more able to assist those in his or her stewardship in their own quest for exaltation. Although this training was given to leaders, members of the Church would do well to learn and emulate these ideals. Calls to leadership and the need for this knowledge may come without warning. Thus, it is up to the individual to make their own preparations for service as they strive for exaltation.

BLESSED ARE THE PERSECUTED

Blessed are they which are persecuted for righteousness sake: for theirs is the kingdom of heaven. (Matthew 5:10)

The last category of the leadership principles or Beatitudes introduced by the Savior in the Sermon on the Mount but the first one explained is "blessed are the persecuted." It appears that Christ began with something familiar; the concept of the righteous being persecuted was not new to Christ's disciples. History has shown that God's prophets have often suffered at the hands of the wicked as gospel truths are taught. The Apostles had the records of Jeremiah who was put in stocks by other religious leaders (see Jeremiah 20:2), faced a mob (see Jeremiah 26:8–9), and according to tradition, was stoned to death (see Bible Dictionary, p. 711). Another prophet, Daniel, was thrown into a lions' den (see Daniel 6) and a furnace (see Daniel 3) while in Babylon as a result of other governmental leaders' machinations. Joseph was sold into slavery by his brothers (see Genesis 37) and then thrown into prison (see Genesis 39).

This pattern of persecution was also present in the Americas. On the way to their promised land, Nephi was beaten and bound by his older brothers on several occasions (see 1 Nephi 3:28; 7:16; 2 Nephi 5—*these quotes are from the Book of Mormon, a religious record of two civilizations recorded by prophets of God in the Americas. Other quotes not recognizable to the reader will be from this book of scripture).* Once in the New World, the righteous were forced to flee into the wilderness to escape destruction (see 2 Nephi 5). A later prophet, Abinadi, was pursued and burned to death at the stake for his persistence in teaching the truth (see Mosiah 17). Then, just before Christ's birth in Palestine, all Christians were given a death sentence if they would not renounce the Savior (see 3 Nephi 1).

With all this history in mind, when he announced this topic to the American disciples, Christ said,

> And blessed are all they who are persecuted for my names sake, for theirs is the Kingdom of heaven. (3 Nephi 12:10)

At the time this sermon was first given, Christ's ministry was just beginning in Palestine and apostasy was the rule. If the Savior declared to the Jews that the reward for those persecuted on his behalf was the kingdom of heaven, he would have been stoned. The statement quoted from 3 Nephi would have been considered blasphemy: Christ, as a mortal man, was placing himself on the level of God. Even his Palestinian disciples might have participated in the execution for they had not yet been fully converted. Much training and teaching had to be accomplished and ordinances to be received before church leaders would be prepared for the task before them. But in the Americas, where apostasy was not complete, many had not forgotten the meaning behind the Laws of Moses. They understood that Christ was the Son of God, the source of salvation, and persecution which came from obedience to his commandments was for righteousness's sake.

The reward for this beatitude is the receipt of the kingdom of heaven, with the kingdom of heaven being understood to mean God's kingdom or the Celestial kingdom. It should also be noted that just enduring persecution does not excuse an individual from complying with the requirements of exaltation, nor will a person be given entrance if they neglect their duties but are persecuted anyway. Christ has stated that those who enter his kingdom are

> they... who received the testimony of Jesus, and believed on his name and were baptized after the manner of his burial, being buried in the water in his name, and this according to the commandment which he has given—
>
> That by keeping the commandments they might be washed and cleansed from all their sins, and receive the Holy Spirit by the laying on of the hands of him who is ordained and sealed unto this power;
>
> And who overcome by faith, and are sealed by the Holy Spirit of promise, which the Father sheds forth upon all those who are just and true. (Doctrine and Covenants 76: 51–53)

Thus, entrance into the kingdom of heaven comes from obedience to the laws of God and acceptance of proper ordinances, not persecution alone. But, in this training, Christ wanted his disciples to be aware that persecution often comes to those who maintain, defend, and comply with God's commandments and ordinances.

Warning

After introducing this principle, the Savior continued his teachings and outlined how those who endure persecution for his sake would receive the kingdom of heaven. In these instructions, Christ compared his disciples with the prophets of old and mentioned several methods of persecution they could expect to face. Then, he identified several areas to be followed by the disciples if they or those of the Church were to enter the kingdom of heaven. If one adhered to these standards, one could expect opposition or persecution. The Savior's warning was

> Blessed are ye, when men shall revile you, and persecute you, and shall say all manner of evil against you falsely, for my sake.
> Rejoice, and be exceeding glad: for great is your reward in heaven: for so persecuted they the prophets which were before you." (Matthew 5:11–12; see also 3 Nephi 12:11–12)

Luke, in his Gospel, also recorded a portion of the Sermon on the Mount. Because the purpose of his book was not the same as Matthew's purpose, it was expressed with a different perspective. Luke recorded,

> Blessed are ye, when men shall hate you, and when they shall separate you from their company, and shall reproach you, and cast out your name as evil, for the Son of man's sake.
> Rejoice ye in that day, and leap for joy: for, behold, your reward is great in heaven: for in the like manner did their fathers unto the prophets. (Luke 6:22–23)

In their callings, the Apostles were to be special witnesses of Christ. Thus, as they bore testimony of his divinity and mission and as they obeyed and were examples of his teachings, they could expect humiliation, false accusations, ostracism, torture, and other persecutions from their countrymen.

This statement or warning was fulfilled soon after the Savior's ascension to heaven. Stephen, a man full of faith and the spirit (see Acts 6:5), was stoned to death after doing great wonders and miracles in the name of Christ (see Acts 7:57–60). Paul, himself a persecutor of Christians before his conversion, after he spent years in service and hardship, was taken to Rome and killed (see Bible Dictionary, p. 742–743). Peter, who was the leader of Christ's Church after the Savior ascended into heaven, suffered martyrdom in Rome at approximately the same time as Paul. The Apostles from Christ's mortal ministry endured torture, stoning, and crucifixion. Only John the Beloved was spared death.

But persecution of the righteous is not limited to the past. In modern times, at the hands of a supposedly more civilized society, there was intense persecution of the followers of Christ which culminated in the martyrdom of Joseph and Hyrum Smith. Then, the Saints were exiled to the West. But that didn't end the persecution and trials. The witnesses of Christ have often faced ridicule and economic hardships besides physical abuse.

Regardless of which tool or method used by Satan to oppose Christ and his kingdom, persecution is one of the indicators that truth is being taught. Hence, when persecution comes, the leaders of Christ's Church should rejoice because it is a sign they are following the path of truth. By enduring persecution in obedience and diligence, as the prophets of old, one can expect to receive the great reward promised.

Salt of the Earth

With this warning and encouragement given, Christ went on to introduce several aspects or ideals of the leadership Church leaders needed to understand and live. If they followed his teachings, they could expect to enter the kingdom of heaven and would be able to assist those in their stewardship obtain exaltation. The Savior said,

> Ye are the salt of the earth: but if the salt have lost his savor, wherewith shall it be salted? It is thenceforth good for

nothing, but to be cast out, and to be trodden under foot of men. (Matthew 5:13; see also 3 Nephi 12:13)

At the time these instructions were given, salt was used as a preservative in the curing of meats and was a crucial element in sustaining life. Besides the use for food storage, this substance had other advantages. Food takes on the characteristics, flavor, or taste of salt when mingled. It was also specified as a token of sacrifice, which made it a vital part in worship (see Leviticus 2:13; Numbers 18:19).

All of these uses made this substance much sought after, and an industry grew from its mining and distribution. As men sought for this item, they found there were areas that seemed to be salt but were impure. It was quickly learned that even though the appearance was correct, the ability to preserve or transform food was not present. Nor was it worthy of sacrifice. Thus, it was fit only to be thrown away.

In their roles as special witnesses of Christ, the Apostles of Palestine and disciples in America had the assignment to preserve the Church that Christ had established just as salt preserves certain foods. What set this organization apart then and does so now are the doctrines, the priesthood, and the ordinances. If any of these areas were to become corrupted, the organization would cease to have the ability to fulfill its mission of exalting God's children. Hence, it would be like all other religions worshipped by man: fruitless and without power.

On another occasion, the Savior said,

> For everyone shall be salted with fire, and every sacrifice shall be salted with salt.
> Salt is good: but if the salt have lost his saltness, wherewith will ye season it? Have salt in yourselves, and have peace one with another. (Mark 9:49–50)

Luke also recorded,

> Then certain of them came to him, saying, Good Master, we have Moses and the prophets, and whosoever shall live by them, shall he not have life?
>
> And Jesus answered, saying, Ye know not Moses, neither the prophets; for if you had known them, ye would have believed on me; for to this intent they were written. For I am sent that ye might have life. Therefore I will liken it unto salt which is good.
>
> But if the salt has lost its savor, wherewith shall it be seasoned? (Luke 14:35–37 JST)

In the latter days, after the Saints had been driven from their homes in Jackson County, Missouri, the Lord revealed to the prophet Joseph Smith that

> when men are called unto mine everlasting gospel, and covenant with an everlasting covenant, they are accounted as the salt of the earth and the savor of men;
>
> They are called to be the savor of men; therefore, if that salt of the earth lose its savor, behold, it is thenceforth good for nothing only to be cast out and trodden under the feet of men. (Doctrine and Covenants 101:39–40)

A modern apostle, Elder James E. Talmage (*apostles in this time are called in the same manner they were called by Christ—by revelation from God*), in his great work *Jesus the Christ* commented on the Savior's teaching to be the salt of the earth. He wrote,

> "Ye are the salt of the earth," said He [Christ]. Salt is the great preservative; as such it has had practical use since very

ancient times. Salt was prescribed as an essential addition to every meat offering under the Mosaic Law. Long before the time of Christ, the use of salt had been accorded a symbolism of fidelity, hospitality, and covenant. To be of use salt must be pure; to be of any saving virtue as salt, it must be salt indeed, and not the product of chemical alteration or of earthy mixture, whereby its saltiness or "savor" would be lost, and, as worthless stuff, it would be fit only to be thrown away. Against such change of faith, against such admixture with the sophistries, so-called philosophies, and heresies of the times, the disciples were especially warned. (*Jesus the Christ*, p. 232–233)

From these scriptures and quote it is apparent that by accepting the doctrines, the priesthood, and the ordinances of the gospel, the Saints become the salt of the earth. Members, and especially leaders, are to maintain all that Christ has taught and preserve the truth in its purity. As this is done, lives take on the characteristics of the gospel like food takes on the characteristics of salt; lives are exalted. But if apostasy or corruption creep in, the savor is lost. The Church, if corrupted, may have the appearance of providing exaltation, but it would be like all the others, ineffective and fit only to be discarded.

In modern times, the Lord warned of the danger of apostasy also using the salt analogy. He told the Prophet Joseph Smith,

> And by hearkening to observe all the words which I, the Lord their God, shall speak unto them, they shall never cease to prevail until the kingdoms of the world are subdued under my feet, and the earth is given unto the saints, to possess it forever and ever.

> But inasmuch as they keep not my commandments, and hearken not to observe all my words, the kingdoms of the world shall prevail against them.
>
> For they were set to be a light unto the world, and to be the saviors of men;
>
> And inasmuch as they are not the saviors of men, they are as salt that has lost its savor, and is therefore good for nothing but to be cast out and trodden under foot of men. (Doctrine and Covenants 103:7–10)

By remaining steadfast and fulfilling their responsibilities in maintaining Church standards, performing the ordinances, and keeping doctrines pure, the leaders of Christ's Church are the salt of the earth. They transform the world as salt transforms food. But Christ warned his leaders that they would face persecution. They would be reviled as harsh and unbending and as being exclusive and elitist, following a course which would prevent many from receiving their rightful reward. During persecution, God would be present with his Saints, adding his strength to theirs. But if the commandments are not observed and the doctrines are not kept pure, God's strength would be withdrawn, and the kingdoms of the earth would prevail over those who professed to be God's people. Thus, for the kingdom of heaven to be obtained, the doctrines of the gospel had to be kept pure and the commandments obeyed.

City on a Hill

The Savior continued his instructions,

> Ye are the light of the world. A city that is set on a hill cannot be hid.

> Neither do men light a candle, and put it under a bushel, but on a candlestick; and it giveth light unto all that are in the house.
>
> Let your light so shine before men, that they may see your good works, and glorify your father which is in heaven. (Matthew 5:14–16)

In the Americas, the Savior said,

> Verily, verily, I say unto you, I give unto you to be the light of this people. A city that is set on a hill cannot be hid.
>
> Behold, do men light a candle and put it under a bushel? Nay, but on a candlestick, and it giveth light to all that are in the house;
>
> Therefore let your light so shine before this people, that they may see your good works and glorify your Father who is in heaven. (3 Nephi 12:14–16)

In his ministry, Christ often used analogies or parables to emphasize his point. In this instance, the leaders of Christ's Church were compared to a city set on a hill and a candle. The leaders in Palestine were to be the light of the world while those in America were a light for their people. There is a difference in the magnitude of their calls, yet both carry the same responsibility.

During the meridian of time, cities were placed where resources were available and could easily be defended. Most often this location was on a hillside overlooking the surrounding area. This additional height would allow the defenders ample time to reach their posts once an enemy had been sighted.

Candles, when lit, would be placed on a candlestick then positioned in locations where all could benefit. It would be self-defeating and perhaps even a little dangerous to place a lit candle under a bushel.

By teaching and obeying the doctrines of God in purity, these leaders would be visible examples of the gospel's power. Their example of good works, living Christ's teachings, and receiving the exalting ordinances should not be hid for they were the light of the world. Although the temptation to withdraw to remote areas to avoid persecution would be present, it had to be fought. This would be like placing a lit candle under a bushel. The light of the gospel had to shine forth so that the honest in heart would know the source of truth and exaltation.

After discussing the salt of the earth, Elder Talmage said,

> Then, changing the figure, Jesus likened them [Church leaders] to the light of the world, and enjoined upon them the duty of keeping their light before the people, as prominently as stands a city built upon a hill, to be seen from all directions, a city that cannot be hid. Of what service would a lighted candle be if hidden under a tub or a box? "Let your light so shine before men," said He, "that they may see your good works, and glorify your Father which is in heaven." (*Jesus the Christ*, p. 233)

Again, as the leaders went about their responsibilities to teach the gospel, they were not to have a false impression. They could expect ridicule and scorn from the world because they were the most visible of Christ's followers. Nevertheless, they were to let their good works testify of and glorify God who is in heaven.

Although persecution is not a pleasant experience, the Lord can use it for the benefit of the individual enduring the trial, his kingdom, and his people. In the April 2001 General Conference, Elder Richard G. Scott (*another modern Apostle*) gave a positive example of how the Lord can use persecution. He spoke of watching a young man as he grew and how his parents taught him to live the commandments of God. The parents encouraged the development of discipline and sacrifice to obtain worthy goals. Swimming was chosen to help instill these qualities in the young man's character. He practiced and sacrificed. Over time, he excelled. But he had one rule: he would keep the Sabbath day holy; he would not compete on Sunday.

Challenges arose. There was a championship meet on Sunday. People questioned whether this young man would hold true to his commitment to obey the law of the Sabbath. Teammates pressured him to compete, but he would not yield. The rejection of friends and the pressure of peers brought sadness and tears. He learned firsthand the reality of Paul's counsel to Timothy that "all that will live godly in Christ Jesus shall suffer persecution" (2 Timothy 3:12). (Refer to *Ensign*, May 2001, p. 8 for the complete story. *The* Ensign *is a monthly publication by The Church of Jesus Christ of Latter-day Saints.*)

For the lessons to be learned, there is a price to be paid. The young man in Elder Scott's example benefited from his service and diligence, from enduring the tears and sorrow of persecution. This young man created a consistent pattern of righteous living and developed a character of strength and capacity of righteousness. As a missionary, he was respected by his peers for his ability to work, his unwavering devotion, and his determination to share the gospel of Christ. The person who had once been rejected by his friends became a respected leader.

This example shows how a leader can be like a candle and a city on a hill. As this young man maintained the standards of the gospel, lives were influenced. He gained the respect of his friends by remaining true to his principles and, in doing so, strengthened those around him.

The Prophet Joseph Smith experienced persecution in many forms. He was beaten, separated from family and friends, reviled, tarred and feathered, and imprisoned. While incarcerated in Liberty, Missouri, Joseph went to the Lord and prayed for help. He wondered why the Lord had not stopped the harsh persecutions the saints were experiencing at the time. The Lord responded by saying,

> And if thou shouldst be cast into the pit, or into the hands of murderers, and the sentence of death passed upon thee; if thou be cast into the deep; if the billowing surge conspire against thee; if fierce winds become thine enemy; if the heavens gather blackness, and all the elements combine to hedge up the way; and above all, if the very jaws of hell shall gape open the mouth wide after thee, know thou, my son, that all these things shall give thee experience, and shall be for thy good. (Doctrine and Covenants 122:7)

On another occasion and in that same prison, the Lord gave comfort to the Prophet Joseph and said,

> My son, peace be unto thy soul; thine adversity and thine afflictions shall be but a small moment;
> And then, if thou endure it well, God shall exalt thee on high; thou shalt triumph over all thy foes. (Doctrine and Covenants 121:7–8)

Persecution may come because the righteous are visible examples of the gospel, of being a city on a hill. Or it may come as a result of maintaining the purity of doctrines and ordinances. But, while painful, this trial will be turned by the Lord into good. Regardless of the reason, if persecution for Christ's name's sake is endured well, God will exalt the persecuted. They receive the kingdom of heaven.

Law of Moses

Another source of persecution Christ's Apostles would face in the meridian of time would come as a result of the law of Moses. This is because most of the population in Palestine followed these laws without understanding their intent. The Savior said,

> Think not that I am come to destroy the law, or the prophets: I am not come to destroy, but to fulfill.
>
> For verily I say unto you, Till heaven and earth pass, one jot or tittle shall in no wise pass from the law, till all be fulfilled.
>
> Whosoever, therefore, shall break one of these least commandments, and shall teach men so to do, he shall in no wise be saved in the Kingdom of heaven; but whosoever shall do and teach
>
> These commandments of the law until it be fulfilled, the same shall be called great, and shall be saved in the Kingdom of heaven.
>
> For I say unto you; That except your righteousness shall exceed the righteousness of the scribes and Pharisees, ye shall in no case enter into the Kingdom of heaven. (Matthew 5:17–20 JST)

The timing of events makes a difference. Because the Sermon in Palestine was given at the beginning of his mortal ministry, many events had yet to take place. The law of Moses had to be fulfilled and obeyed until the Atonement was completed. Those who failed to obey the commandments and taught others to do likewise would not be exalted in God's kingdom.

On the American continent, the people of Nephi faced a peculiar circumstance after the sign of Christ's birth. A small group of people contended that observance of the law of Moses was no longer necessary because the Savior had entered mortality.

> But it came to pass that they soon became converted, and were convinced of the error which they were in, for it was made known unto them that the law was not yet fulfilled, and that it must be fulfilled in every whit; yea, the word came unto them that it must be fulfilled; yea, that one jot or tittle should not pass away till it should all be fulfilled; therefore in this same year were they brought to a knowledge of their error and did confess their faults. (3 Nephi 1:25)

Disobedience to the commandments of God which were in force would result in the consequences of the law: the sinner would be barred from God's kingdom. On the other hand, the façade of obedience was not a guarantee that a person would receive exaltation. This is what the Savior was referring to when he required the Apostles to exceed the righteousness of the Scribes and Pharisees. Unless they looked beyond the letter of the law to its meaning, to be spiritually reborn and develop God-like attributes, the Apostles would fail. The leaders of the Jewish nation at that time obeyed and observed the sacrifices as prescribed by the Lord yet failed to recognize that the purpose of these rites were to direct people to the Lamb of God. The Savior pointed this dissonance out in a very plain manner as recorded in Luke 14:35–37 JST, quoted previous. Although there would come a time when the Mosaic law was fulfilled and new ordinances established, portions of the law of Moses would continue until their fulfillment.

After his death and resurrection, the Savior taught his disciples in the Americas:

> Think not that I am come to destroy the law or the prophets. I am not come to destroy but to fulfill;
>
> For verily I say unto you, one jot nor one tittle hath not passed away from the law, but In me it hath all been fulfilled.
>
> And behold, I have given you the law and the commandments of my Father, that ye Shall believe in me, and that ye shall repent of your sins, and come unto me with a broken heart And a contrite spirit. Behold, ye have the commandments before you, and the law is fulfilled.
>
> Therefore come unto me and be ye saved; for verily I say unto you, that except ye shall keep my commandments, which I have commanded you at this time, ye shall in no case enter into the Kingdom of heaven. (3 Nephi 12:17–20)

In relation to the law of Moses, Elder Talmage wrote,

> That they should make no error as to the relationship of the ancient law and the gospel of the kingdom which He was elucidating, Jesus assured them [Church leaders] that He had not come to destroy the law nor to nullify the teachings and predictions of the prophets, but to fulfill such and to establish that for which the developments of the centuries gone had been but preparatory. The gospel may be said to have destroyed the Mosaic law only as the seed is destroyed in the growth of the new plant, only as the bud

is destroyed by the bursting forth of the rich, full, and fragrant flowers, only as infancy and youth pass forever as the maturity of years develops. Not a jot or a tittle of the law was to be void. A more effective analogy than the last could scarcely have been conceived; the jot or yod, and the tittle, were small literary marks in the Hebrew script; for present purposes we may regard them as equivalent to the dot of an "i" or the cross of a "t"; with the first, the jot, our English word 'iota,' signifying a trifle, is related. Not even the least commandment could be violated without penalty; but the disciples were admonished to take heed that their keeping of the commandments was not after the manner of the scribes and Pharisees, whose observance was that of ceremonial externalism, lacking the essentials of genuine devotion; for they were assured that by such an insincere course they could "in no case enter into the kingdom of heaven." (*Jesus the Christ*, p. 233-234)

The entire purpose of the law of Moses, with all its observances and commandments, was to point men to Christ, to help them recognize the Creator when he came, for all must believe in him, repent of their sins, and come unto him with a broken heart and a contrite spirit to enter God's kingdom. At the point this training was given in the Americas, Christ was a resurrected being. His mortal assignment had been completed and by that most of the law of Moses fulfilled. Since sacrifices as specified by the law of Moses were no longer necessary, Christ instructed the leaders of his Church in the land Bountiful to keep the commandments and ordinances he had given them. Obedience was and still is necessary to gain the kingdom of heaven.

As they obeyed his commandments, Christ's disciples on both continents were warned to expect persecution and ridicule. In Jerusalem, after the Savior left, the unconverted would believe the Jewish Christians had betrayed the faith of their fathers. By not adhering to the law of Moses, the Christians were guilty of blasphemy and merited the consequences of that sin.

The aspect of this principle which can be inferred for modern leaders in the Church is that of following cultural laws and practices so long as they do not conflict with the gospel. Christ's disciples are not to alienate those whom they are attempting to serve. Since there are plenty of areas from which contention and persecution can arise, additional reasons should not be given. In this sense they are to "render therefore unto Caesar the things which are Caesar's; and unto God the things that are God's" (see Matthew 22:21). However, practices and traditions which conflict with gospel teachings are to be discarded. It is in this area that persecution may arise.

Summary

All leaders in Christ's Church can expect to experience persecution at one time or another as they discharge their duties with diligence. Some will disparage and ridicule leaders from within the Church while others will criticize and ostracize from without. Some persecution will arise from those who consider tradition and culture more important than truth. Care must be taken to avoid offending local law or culture when the law and culture do not conflict with the commandments and teachings of God. The leaders of Christ's Church are to be as a city on a hill, defending the Savior's teachings when necessary, and as a candle, shining the light of the kingdom. They become the salt of the earth to preserve the exalting doctrines and ordinances of the gospel, to help the world adjust to Christ's teachings, and to not accept the world's ideas. As a reward for their diligence in obedience and endurance in persecution, the Apostles in Palestine, the disciples in the Americas, and the leaders in other times and places would qualify for the kingdom of heaven.

In essence, leaders are to live and defend their beliefs. President Gordon B. Hinckley (*a modern-day prophet*) stated,

> It takes resolution to be virtuous when those around you scoff at virtue.
>
> It takes commitment to abstain from harmful substances when those around you scoff at sobriety and at being free from drugs.
>
> It takes courage to be a man or woman of integrity when those around you forsake gospel principles for expediency or convenience.
>
> It takes love in our hearts to speak in peaceful testimony of the divinity of the Lord Jesus Christ to those who would mock Him and belittle and demean Him.
>
> There will be times that demand courage for each of us because disciples of the Lord are to live with their consciences. Disciples of the Lord are to live with their principles. Disciples of the Lord are to live with their convictions. Each of us is to live with his or her testimony. (*Ensign*, September 2001, p. 4–5)

Many years earlier, the Prophet Joseph Smith pointed out that the righteous saints should expect to experience persecution. He said,

> The enemies of this people will never get weary of their persecution against the Church, until they are overcome. I

expect they will array everything against me that is in their power to control, and that we shall have a long and tremendous warfare. He that will war the true Christian warfare against the corruptions of these last days will have wicked men and angels of devils, and all the internal powers of darkness continually arrayed against him. When wicked and corrupt men oppose, it is a criterion to judge if a man is warring the Christian warfare. When all men speak evil of you falsely, blessed are ye. Shall a man be considered bad, when men speak evil of him? No. If a man stands and opposes the world of sin, he may expect to have all wicked and corrupt spirits arrayed against him. But it will be but a little season, and all these afflictions will be turned away from us, inasmuch as we are faithful, and are not overcome by these evils. By seeing the blessings of the endowment rolling on, and the Kingdom increasing and spreading from sea to sea, we shall rejoice that we were not overcome by these foolish things. (*Teachings of the Prophet Joseph Smith*, p. 259)

BLESSED ARE THE PEACEMAKERS

Blessed are the peacemakers: for they shall be called the children of God.
(Matthew 5:9; 3 Nephi 12:9)

While studying the Sermon on the Mount, it is easy to recognize the instructions and concepts taught about enduring persecution. This is because the ideals for that principle were presented immediately after the topic was introduced. The apparent lack of explanation for the other Beatitudes could lead to the conclusion that being persecuted is the paramount subject. But that conclusion would be wrong. The other Beatitudes are just as important and are explained, but their explanation occurs after that of being persecuted and in reverse order of being introduced.

In the second-to-last leadership principle mentioned, that of being peacemakers, Christ taught the importance of removing anger and contention from the lives of the leaders of his Church. Just as the idea of the righteous having to endure persecution was known, the concept of avoiding contention was not a major revelation for God's people. Over a hundred years before Christ was born, the American prophet Alma commanded his people that there should be no contention one with another, but that they should look forward with one eye, having one faith and one baptism, having their hearts knit together in unity and in love one towards another. (Mosiah 18:21)

Besides being told to avoid anger and contention, the Saints were told to be unified in their faith and in their observance of the ordinances. They were to be unified in love. After he had descended from the heavens and before he began this leadership training in the Americas, Christ taught the multitude:

For verily, verily I say unto you, he that hath the spirit of contention is not of me, but is of the devil, who is the father of contention, and he stirreth up the hearts of men to contend with anger, one with another.

Behold, this is not my doctrine, to stir up the hearts of men with anger, one against another; but this is my doctrine, that such things should be done away. (3 Nephi 11:29–30)

Contention and anger are to be avoided because they come from Satan. Those who give way to those emotions are on the path toward being a disciple of the adversary for they are listening to his spirit. After the Savior's resurrection and ascension into heaven, this teaching was kept before the Saints. The Apostle James wrote a general letter to the twelve tribes of Israel and said that the "fruit of righteousness is sown in peace of them that make peace" (James 3:18). In more recent years, the Lord told the Prophet Joseph Smith,

And this I do that I may establish my gospel, that there may not be so much contention; yea, Satan doth stir up the hearts of the people to contention concerning the points of my doctrine; and in these things they do err, for they do wrest the scriptures and do not understand them. (Doctrine and Covenants 10:63)

Peace and righteousness come together. The gospel was established to exalt God's children and that requires contention to be avoided. When conflicts erupt over doctrine and protocol, speculating on items that have no bearing on the exaltation of God's children, it is a result of Satan's efforts and causes the Spirit of God to depart. But arguments over doctrine and the loss of the Spirit is not the only concern. The appearance of contention is a sign that faith in Christ is weak or gone. In *Lectures on Faith*, the Prophet Joseph Smith said, "That men, as soon as they lose their faith, run into strifes, contentions, darkness, and difficulties" (*Lectures on Faith*, Lecture Seventh, p. 68).

Elder M. Russell Ballard addressed the idea of peace in the April 2002 General Conference. He pointed out that "wickedness never was happiness" (Alma 41:10). There is no peace in sin, vulgarity, promiscuity, addiction to drugs, alcohol, or pornography. There is no peace in being contentious or abusive. These individuals will remain in mental and spiritual turmoil until they turn to Christ in humility and seek forgiveness through sincere and complete repentance (refer to *Ensign*, May 2002, p. 87–88).

Over the centuries, the Savior has taught that for the Church of Christ to be successful in assisting God's children in their quest to know God and achieve exaltation, true peace had to be present. Contention must be eliminated, and faith must be increased. As the scriptures have shown, Satan has his own designs and objectives. He will bend all his efforts to create dissension and contention among the Church in matters of protocol or doctrine, and thus, people will reject the counsel of the Savior's chosen leaders and neglect the sacred and necessary ordinances.

It is Satan's ultimate desire to prevent the exaltation of as many of his brothers and sisters as possible.

In order for God's children to achieve exaltation, efforts made by the leaders of Christ's Church can be pivotal. By maintaining the new and everlasting covenant, leaders can build and strengthen the faith of those in their stewardship. They can strengthen the peace between members. As the gospel spreads and God's commandments are obeyed, peace grows. Elder Ballard continued his instructions in Conference and said that only when gospel principles are understood and lived can peace be distilled in the hearts of God's children. For "he who doeth the works of righteousness shall receive his reward, even peace in this world, and eternal life in the world to come" (Doctrine and Covenants 59:23).

True peace comes only through faith in Jesus Christ and obedience to the gospel of Christ. Thus, as leaders promote faith and obedience to the laws and commandments of God, they "shall be called the children of Christ, his sons, and his daughters; for behold, this day he hath spiritually begotten you; for ye say that your hearts are changed through faith on his name; therefore, ye are born of him and have become his sons and his daughters" (Mosiah 5:7).

In accordance with the principle of being a peacemaker, Elder Bruce R. McConkie wrote,

> The gospel of peace makes men children of God! Christ came to bring peace—peace on earth and good will to men. His gospel gives peace in this world and eternal life in the world to come. He is the prince of peace. How beautiful upon the mountains are the feet of them who preach the gospel of peace, who say unto Zion: Thy God reigneth! Let there be peace on earth and let it begin with his saints. By

this shall all men know the Lord's disciples: They are peacemakers; they seek to compose difficulties; they hate war and love peace; they invite all men to forsake evil, overcome the world, flee from avarice and greed, stand in holy places, and receive for themselves that peace which passeth understanding, that peace which comes only by the power of the Spirit.

And these are they who are adopted into the family of God. They become the sons and daughters of him whose we are. They are born again. They take upon themselves a new name, the name of their new Father, the name of Christ. Those who believe in him have power to become his sons and his daughters. Truly the peacemakers shall be called the children of God! (*The Mortal Messiah* 2:123–124)

A peacemaker, as he or she is obedient, puts on Christ and is adopted into God's family to become a son or daughter of the Savior. A peacemaker is not just a son or daughter but is an actual heir of God. In an effort to explain how this occurs, Paul wrote to the Galatians that

ye are all the children of God by faith in Christ Jesus.

For as many of you as have been baptized into Christ have put on Christ. . . .

And because ye are sons, God hath sent forth the Spirit of his Son into your hearts, crying, Abba, Father.

Wherefore thou art no more a servant, but a son; and if a son, then an heir of God through Christ. (Galatians 3:26–27; 4:6–7)

Once again, the Savior points his people toward the whole purpose of existence—exaltation. Therefore, as children of God and heirs of that divine nature, it is our responsibility to develop faith in God and to learn and assume the attributes of our Father, one of which is to be a peacemaker. Those who add the ideals of being a peacemaker to all the other ideals being taught during this training meeting and receive the exalting ordinances under the hands of those with the proper authority will obtain all that the Father has.

As he taught, the Savior identified several ideals which make being peacemakers so important. These concepts deal with suppressing anger, reconciling differences, meeting obligations, and coming to appropriate compromises. By following the Savior's teachings, the leaders of his Church will be called the children of God, for they truly are peacemakers.

Anger

In the training for this principle, the Savior began by reiterating the Mosaic law against murder.

> Ye have heard that it was said by them of old time, Thou shalt not kill; and whosoever shall kill shall be in danger of the judgment. (Matthew 5:21)

The Savior was a little more descriptive when this idea was taught in the Americas.

> Ye have heard that it hath been said by them of old time, and it is also written before you, that thou shalt not kill, and whosoever shall kill shall be in danger of the judgment of God. (3 Nephi 12:21)

For a person who is striving to be a peacemaker, "thou shalt not kill" seems to be self-evident. Yet the Savior recognized that the murder act is but an end result of the actual problem. Disdaining the approach that is most often used, that of treating the symptom, the Savior determined to concentrate on the cause: anger. Christ continued,

> But I say unto you, That whosoever is angry with his brother shall be in danger of the judgment: and whosoever shall say to his brother, Raca, shall be in danger of the council: but whosoever shall say, Thou fool, shall be in danger of hell fire. (Matthew 5:22 JST; see also 3 Nephi 12:22)

For leaders of God's kingdom (parents are included in this category), the destructive emotion of anger must be bridled for it can lead to catastrophic consequences. When anger is present and is not suppressed, words may be said that are hurtful, driving those with weaker testimonies from the gospel or family, making the speaker at least partially responsible for the consequences. If anger is allowed action, property may be damaged or an innocent third party could be killed or seriously injured. But the property loss and physical injuries that may result from anger might be considered secondary because injuries will be made whole if only through the Resurrection. The loss of faith by a member or loss of a family member, when observing a leader or parent act or speak in anger, can have eternal consequences. Because of this consequence, those who give vent to anger are in danger of judgment or condemnation if repentance is not made.

The Savior continued and mentioned that if someone is contemptuous or derisive of another, they could be subject to the decisions or pronouncements of the local civic leaders. Under the law of Moses there were legal or social consequences prescribed for acting out in anger and the council was charged with upholding the law. In taking the training of those who would be leaders a step further, the Savior revealed that those who speak in anger and do not repent would also be in danger of eternal damnation because of the loss of faith.

Thousands of years after Christ, as he instructed the Saints about anger, the prophet Brigham Young said that

> if you give way to your angry feelings, it sets on fire the whole course of nature, and is set on fire of hell; and you are then apt to set those on fire who are contending with you. When you feel as though you would burst, tell the old boiler to burst, and just laugh at the temptation to speak evil. If you will continue to do that, you will soon be masters of yourselves as to be able, if not to tame, to control your tongues—able to speak when you ought, and to be silent when you ought. (*Discourses of Brigham Young*, p. 269)

As President Young taught, anger causes a like emotion in others. For that reason, the Saints were to suppress their anger and not speak evil. By so doing, the individual becomes stronger—a master of self—while the Spirit of God remains and faith is strengthened.

The loss of faith in members of Christ's Church as a result of intemperate words or actions is not the only issue. Anger and contention are of the devil. When a leader succumbs to anger, he or she loses the Spirit of God which is so important to meeting God's objectives.

Elder George Q. Cannon, another early Church leader, wrote,

> The Spirit of God produces peace and quiet and good temper. Men and women who have the Spirit are amiable, are kind and loving one towards another. They control their tempers because the Spirit of God will not dwell where the spirit of anger and hatred and violence exist.
>
> We should, of all people upon the face of the earth, be the best tempered, the kindest, the most forebearing, the

most loving, the least disposed to quarrel. (*Gospel Truth*, p. 44)

Contention and anger are of the devil. When a leader acts in anger, the faith of those in his or her stewardship could be injured or destroyed. But just as important, the leader will lose the Spirit of the Lord as an assistant. By keeping a firm grip on anger, the Spirit of God is retained and faith is strengthened. Thus, we become the best tempered, the kindest, the most loving of peoples. Peace reigns.

Reconciliation

Besides keeping one's own anger in check, a leader must do all in his or her power to resolve the differences between themselves and members of their stewardship. By doing this reconciliation, anger is stopped from developing in others. The Lord said,

> Therefore if thou bring thy gift to the altar, and there rememberest that thy brother hath ought against thee;
> Leave there thy gift before the altar, and go thy way; first be reconciled to thy brother, and then come and offer thy gift. (Matthew 5:23-24)

At the time these instructions were given, a temple existed in Jerusalem. Although Israel, as a people, had fallen into apostasy, temple worship was still recognized as the central point of life. Attendance and participation were considered a social and spiritual necessity.

Even though the temple ordinances were and still are important in achieving exaltation, the Savior wanted his disciples to realize proper priorities. If offense had been given to another or if an offense had been perceived, the Church leader was expected to get the problem resolved before their sacrifices would be accepted by the Father. In this effort, the intent of the sacrifice is as important as the actual event.

This concept of being reconciled to our brothers and sisters before approaching God is not limited to temple ordinances. Although there was a temple in the Americas, the Lord adjusted his teaching to the American Saints:

> Therefore, if ye shall come unto me, or shall desire to come unto me, and rememberest that thy brother hath aught against thee—
>
> Go thy way unto thy brother, and first be reconciled to thy brother, and then come unto me with full purpose of heart, and I will receive you. (3 Nephi 12:23–24)

Unlike the people of Palestine, the American Saints had remembered that the purpose of all the rites, ceremonies, and laws of Moses were to direct people to Christ, the source of Salvation. In the American version of this training, Christ pointed out that if a person desired to come unto the Savior, the relationship with others must be taken care of first: "inasmuch as ye have done it unto one of the least of these my brethren, ye have done it unto me" (see Matthew 25:40).

Although the wording of their training was different, the Church leaders in both areas of the world were taught that if offense had been given, the leader had the responsibility to approach the other party in an attempt at reconciliation. Elder Bruce McConkie in his Messiah series explained that

> if we choose to come unto Christ and to be one with him in his fold; if we bring our gifts to his holy altar, that our wealth and means may be used to further his work on earth;

and if we then remember that others have aught against us, our obligation, more important than the gifts we bestow, is to heal the wounded feelings of our brethren. Jesus speaks here not of our anger or ill feeling towards others, but of their ill feelings, for whatever cause, against us. No matter that we are the one who has been wronged. The gospel standard calls for us to search out those whose anger is kindled against us and to do all in our power to douse the fires of hate and animosity. "Go thy way unto thy brother, and first be reconciled to thy brother," he said to the Nephites, "and then come unto me with full purpose of heart, and I will receive you." (*The Mortal Messiah* 2:137)

Resolving the anger or animosity an individual has toward a Church leader is very important. A bishop, stake president, quorum leader, or parent cannot direct those in his stewardship toward God if the person cannot sustain the leader in his call. Council and direction provided by the leader for the benefit of the kingdom may be overlooked or disregarded if this is the case. Or an individual may elect not to fulfill the responsibilities that come with a call issued by the offending leader. Therefore, a leader in Christ's Church must make allowances, reconcile to douse the fires of animosity, and encourage all to come unto Christ for salvation (see 3 Nephi 12:20).

The Savior gave an example of this ideal later in his ministry when he presented the parable of the prodigal son. Often this parable is used to teach forgiveness of others, but there is an ancillary lesson. In this story, a father has immense wealth and two sons. After a time, the younger son comes forward and requests the division of the inheritance among the sons. This the father does. Upon receiving his portion, the younger son departs. Over the years, this son wastes the inheritance in sinful practices. After he has sunk to the lowest levels, the prodigal returns home to find his father's welcoming embrace. When the older, more dutiful son learns of the festivities for the wayward brother, he is offended and refuses to participate. As soon as the father learned of the older son's anger, he hurried outside to be reconciled (see Luke 15:11–32).

In the April 2002 General Conference, President Thomas S. Monson, the then-current prophet of God, gave two examples of this ideal. The first shows the negative impact on an individual's life when a leader fails to be a peacemaker. President Monson talked about a lifelong friend named Leonard. While Leonard was not a member of the Church, his wife and children were. He lived a clean and worthy life full of service. His family and friends wondered why Leonard had never participated in the blessings the gospel of Christ brings to its members.

In Leonard's later years he suffered from ill health and eventually was hospitalized. In what turned out to be President Monson's last conversation with Leonard, he explained why he'd never joined the Church. Leonard's parents owned a farm and had reached a point where it was necessary to sell. An offer had been tendered and accepted. A neighboring farmer came to Leonard's father and asked that the farm be sold to him, suggesting that he'd be able to watch over it. Leonard's parents agreed and the farm was sold to the neighbor. This neighbor held a responsible position in the Church and the trust this implied help persuade the family to sell to him.

Not long after the sale had been made, the neighbor sold both his own farm and the property acquired from Leonard's family. The combined parcel maximized the value and the selling price. A long-asked question of why Leonard had never joined the Church had been answered. He always felt that his family had been deceived by the neighbor (refer to *Ensign*, May 2002, p. 18–19).

In this example, Leonard felt that a responsible Church leader had betrayed the trust his family had placed in him. Because of that example, this man never joined the Church. If the leader had followed this principle and attempted to reconcile, Leonard may have accepted baptism. As it was, the kingdom was deprived of Leonard's abilities and his family never received the blessings of the temple in mortality.

The second example has a happier ending. It shows how this principle can repair a rift. President Monson knew of a family that came to America from Germany. As with many immigrants, learning the language was difficult.

During this time, their third child was born and then died within two months. The father was a cabinetmaker and fashioned a beautiful casket for the child. On the day of the funeral, the family walked to the chapel with the father carrying the tiny casket. They, with a small number of friends, arrived at the building and found the door was locked. A busy bishop had forgotten about the funeral and was unable to be contacted. With nothing else to do, the father gathered his family and walked back home in the drenching rain, still carrying the precious casket under his arm.

When the bishop learned of his mistake, he visited the family and apologized. Although he'd been deeply hurt, the father accepted the apology and both men embraced. (refer to *Ensign*, May 2002, p. 79)

This concept of attempting reconciliation by those in leadership positions is personified by Elder Spencer W. Kimball. After receiving his call from President J. Reuben Clark, Jr., to be an Apostle,

> Spencer went around to people he had done business with and said, "If you think I have ever taken unfair advantage

of you, please tell me. I want to make it right with you." A couple thought they should have a little more money on some sales, and Spencer paid them what they asked, but all the rest just waved his offer aside. He talked again with the neighbor with whom he had had an old water dispute, and even took flowers. He wanted no bad feelings when he left. (*The Story of Spencer W. Kimball*, p. 68)

Care must be taken to avoid taking this concept to an extreme. Christ was not instructing his leaders to be conciliatory in all things and at all times. Reconciliation may not be possible if the ill feelings an individual is experiencing results from the individual's sins or desire to live outside Gospel standards. As was mentioned in the prior beatitude, a leader is expected to be the salt of the earth and to preserve in purity the ordinances and doctrines as taught by Christ.

In keeping with being a peacemaker, a leader should conduct his or her affairs in such a manner that would be an example rather than a distraction. The Savior instructed that if a leader learns an individual in his or her care has been offended or has given offense, the leader is to be the one to make a serious effort to reconcile.

Compromise/Obligations

After discussing the need to overcome anger and reconciling differences, the Savior discussed the last ideals in his explanation of how a leader is to be a peacemaker. He said,

> Agree with thine adversary quickly, whiles thou art in the way with him; lest at any time the adversary deliver thee to the judge, and the judge deliver thee to the officer, and thou be cast into prison.

Verily I say unto thee, Thou shalt by no means come out thence, till thou hast paid the uttermost farthing." (Matthew 5:25–26; see also 3 Nephi 12:25–26)

At the time of Christ, if an individual had a debt which he was unable to repay, the debtor was thrown into prison. He would remain there until the debt was paid in full either by his family or a benefactor. Most often the debt remained unpaid, and the debtor remained in prison. This practice was used later in the Savior's ministry in a parable teaching the principle of forgiveness (see Matthew 18:23–35). The people in the New World also had a similar method of debt collection.

In the scripture quoted above, the Savior told the leaders of his Church to meet all their obligations. It was understood that if debts of Church leaders were not paid, the enemies of God's kingdom would not hesitate to cast them into prison. With the leaders in prison, the kingdom might falter or pause in its progress.

This council was later taken by the Apostle Paul and passed on to the Saints. In his epistle to the Romans, he wrote,

> But first, render therefore to all their dues, according to custom, tribute to whom tribute, custom to whom custom, that your consecrations may be done in fear to whom fear belongs, and in honor of him to whom honor belongs.
>
> Owe no man anything, but to love one another: for he that loveth another hath fulfilled the law. (Romans 13:7–8)

The payment of debts was also taught in more modern times. The Lord told the Prophet Joseph Smith,

> And again, verily I say unto you, concerning your debts—behold it is my will that you shall pay all your debts." (Doctrine and Covenants 104:78)

An important aspect of being a peacemaker is that of meeting obligations. If a debt is not satisfied, contention arises between the parties involved and can expand to include a Relief Society, a quorum, or a ward. Even today, the Church remains as debt free as possible. Meeting houses, temples, and other religious facilities are built and maintained from the donations of faithful members. Debt is not involved for "the borrower is servant to the lender" (see Proverbs 22:7).

In the modern world, a debtor can avoid prison for the non-payment of financial debts. Even if prison is avoided, the appearance that a Church leader is dishonest or untrustworthy is presented to the world and the progress of the kingdom could be hindered.

With this beatitude, being a peacemaker requires more than avoiding anger, reconciling problems, and meeting obligations. A leader needs to compromise when necessary and under the direction of the Spirit. This is another sense of agreeing with your adversary.

The Old Testament provides an example of this aspect of being a peacemaker. After returning from Egypt a wealthy, Abram (later renamed Abraham) was accompanied by his nephew Lot. The Lord had blessed both men with immense wealth while in Egypt. Their riches were so great that their flocks and herds could not dwell together in the new land (see Genesis 13:5–6). Because of the limited resources, conflict soon broke out between Lot's and Abram's herdsmen (see Genesis 13:7). In an effort to be a peacemaker, Abram used a unique approach. The scriptures record,

> And Abram said unto Lot, Let there be no strife, I pray thee, between me and thee, and between my herdmen and thy herdmen; for we be brethren.
>
> Is not the whole land before thee? Separate thyself, I pray thee, from me: if thou wilt take the left hand, then I will

go to the right; or if thou depart to the right hand, then I will go to the left.

And Lot lifted up his eyes, and beheld all the plain of Jordan, that it was well watered every where, before the Lord destroyed Sodom and Gomorrah, even as the garden of the Lord, like the land of Egypt, as thou comest unto Zoar.

Then Lot chose him all the plain of Jordan; and Lot journeyed east: and they separated themselves the one from the other. (Genesis 13:8–11)

In an agrarian society, land which has water and vegetation is at a premium. Abram and Lot had amassed so much wealth that it was not possible for the land to sustain the herds of both men. Rather than take the best land for himself and worsen the conflict which had developed within the family, Abram was the peacemaker and gave Lot the first choice of land. In essence, Abram gave Lot the best land and thus kept peace in the family. By remaining righteous, he went on to become a patriarch for a great posterity. His reward for this and other examples of obedience was to be adopted into God's family and heir to all God had.

Summary

In teaching the future leaders of his Church how to be peacemakers, the Savior stressed several ideals: avoiding and controlling anger, reconciling differences, and meeting one's obligations or making appropriate compromises. Compliance with each of these ideals help reduce the anger and contention within the Church while building faith in Christ. Christ ended his discussion of this principle by discussing the importance of meeting all obligations. The Savior pointed out that if debts are not met, the debtor causes resentment and distrust which again drives out the Spirit. In the extreme, a leader could be imprisoned, further slowing the work of the kingdom. Coupled with meeting obligations is that of appropriate compromise. Examples were shown of "agreeing with the adversary" to avoid disruption of the work of Christ. In this last ideal, care must be taken to maintain the purity and integrity of the doctrines and ordinances. These items are necessary for the exaltation of God's children and cannot be compromised. All else can be adjusted as needed and under the direction of the Spirit.

The Savior, in this beatitude, taught that a leader reconciling wrongs, real or perceived, helps reduce or remove the source of contention. As the examples have shown, coming to a resolution deepens the bonds of love and trust between members and strengthens the kingdom.

It is desirable for anger to be controlled because that emotion feeds upon itself, drives out the Spirit of God, robs a person of peace, and leads to many other destructive acts. Christ taught that the person who did not control their anger would be subject to judgment. Those who deliberately incited anger in others would be in "danger of hellfire."

The idea of a society living in peace, one with another, may seem a bit idealistic or unattainable. But it has been achieved. The city of Enoch is one such society. Enoch's people lived their lives in accordance with the principles of the gospel and dwelt in righteousness. They were of one heart (see Moses 7:18). After Christ had appeared to the people in the New World, they lived the gospel and saw the results.

> And it came to pass that there was no contention in the land, because of the love of God which did dwell in the hearts of the people.
>
> And there were no envyings, nor strifes, nor tumults, nor whoredoms, nor lyings, nor murders, nor any manner

of lasciviousness; and surely there could not be a happier people among all the people who had been created by the hand of God.

There were no robbers, no murderers, neither were there Lamanites, nor any manner of –ites; but they were in one, the children of Christ, and heirs to the Kingdom of God." (4 Nephi 1:15–17)

As Elder McConkie wrote,

> And these are they who are adopted into the family of God. They become the sons and daughters of him whose we are. They are born again. They take upon themselves a new name, the name of the new Father, the name of Christ. Those who believe in him have power to become his sons and his daughters. Truly the peacemakers shall be called the children of God! (*The Mortal Messiah* 2:124)

BLESSED ARE THE PURE IN HEART

Blessed are the pure in heart: for they shall see God. (Matthew 5:8)

Thus was the sixth beatitude recited in Palestine. When the Savior repeated these instructions to his disciples in the Americas, he made a small addition. He inserted the word "all." With this change, "Blessed are the pure in heart" became "Blessed are all the pure in heart" (see 3 Nephi 12:8). The addition made in the Americas removed any ambiguity or question. God does not bless one righteous individual then withhold those blessings from another. Any and all who comply with the requirements and commandments as outlined by God are the pure in heart and will receive the promised blessing (see Doctrine and Covenants 130:20–21; 82:10).

The blessing for this beatitude, that of seeing God, is not fully comprehended by most of God's children. Those who receive the reward for being pure in heart will not view deity from a distance or enjoy feeling his presence but will experience a more personal and physical visitation. Elder Bruce R. McConkie, an Apostle in modern times, wrote,

> How glorious is the voice we hear from him! Man may see his Maker! Did not Abraham, Isaac, and Jacob see the Lord?

Did not Moses and Aaron, Nadab and Abihu, and seventy of the elders of Israel see the God of Israel, under whose feet was a paved work of a sapphire stone? Was it not thus with Isaiah and Nephi, with Jacob and Moroni, and with mighty prophets without number in all ages? Is God a respecter of persons who will appear to one righteous person and withhold his face from another person of like spiritual stature? Is he not the same yesterday, today, and forever, dealing the same with all people, considering that all souls are equally precious in his sight? Did not Moses seek diligently to sanctify his people, while they were yet in the wilderness, that they might see the face of God and live? Does not the scriptures say that the brother of Jared had such a perfect knowledge of God that he could not be kept from seeing within the veil? Why then shall not the Lord Jesus invite all men to be as the prophets, to purify themselves so as to see the face of the Lord?

"It is written: Verily, thus saith the Lord. It shall come to pass that every soul who forsaketh his sins and cometh unto me, and calleth on my name, and obeyeth my voice, and keepeth my commandments, shall see my face and know that I am." (Doctrine and Covenants 93:1) How glorious the concept is! What a wondrous reality! The pure in heart—all the pure in heart—shall see God!" (*The Mortal Messiah* 2:123).

Prophets throughout the ages have seen God and ancient scriptures record some of their accounts. These writings also record the experiences of righteous men who were not prophets seeing God such the brother of Jared, Aaron, Nabad, Abihu, and seventy elders of Israel. All of these events can be used as examples to show that it is possible for a person to achieve a trigger point of righteousness and faith, of becoming sufficiently pure, so as to have God appear to him or her.

As he had in the prior Beatitudes, Christ continued to point his disciples toward exaltation. Further study of the scriptures show that the requirements which qualify one to be introduced into God's presence also qualify one for the celestial kingdom. But this wonderful experience of entering God's presence and kingdom will be granted only on the Lord's timetable and in his own way. The Savior told the Prophet Joseph Smith,

> Therefore, sanctify yourselves that your minds become single to God, and the days will come that you shall see him; for he will unveil his face unto you, and it shall be in his own time, and in his own way, and according to his own will. (Doctrine and Covenants 88:68)

On another occasion the Lord said,

> And again, verily I say unto you that it is your privilege, and a promise I give unto you that have been ordained unto this ministry, that inasmuch as you strip yourselves from jealousies and fears, and humble yourselves before me, for ye are not sufficiently humble, the veil shall be rent and you shall see me and know that I am—not with the carnal neither natural mind, but with the spiritual. (Doctrine and Covenants 67:10)

These scriptures point out that as individuals, in the incidence of this training, if Church leaders rid themselves of jealousies and fears and develop humility, they will become clean or pure in heart and the veil will be rent. The promise is that those who sanctify themselves by being obedient and faithful shall see God and know that he is. This momentous event can occur during mortality—in temples, in groves, or on a high mountain—but it may not. And if it does not occur during mortality, then the sanctified individual will see God in the celestial kingdom and receive the reward for which his or her efforts qualify. The Prophet Joseph Smith received a vision regarding the rewards that can be received by the pure in heart and wrote that

> they are they who received the testimony of Jesus, and believed on his name and were baptized after the manner of his burial, being buried in the water in his name, and this according to the commandment which he has given—
>
> That by keeping the commandments they might be washed and cleansed from all their sins, and receive the Holy Spirit by the laying on of the hands of him who is ordained and sealed unto this power;
>
> And who overcome by faith, and are sealed by the Holy Spirit of promise, which the Father sheds forth upon all those who are just and true....
>
> These shall dwell in the presence of God and his Christ forever and ever....
>
> These are they whose bodies are celestial, whose glory is that of the sun, even the glory of God, the highest of all, whose glory the sun of the firmament is written of as being typical. (Doctrine and Covenants 76:51–53, 62, 70)

The conclusion is that for a leader (or any other person) in Christ's kingdom to become pure in heart, he or she must obey the commandments of God and receive the necessary ordinances. Paul taught that "the unrighteous shall not inherit the kingdom of God" (see 1 Corinthians 6:9). Those who do not comply with God's requirements will not receive the reward God has reserved for the righteous. In the process outlined by God, the obedient are sanctified and prepared by the Holy Ghost, and then he or she will see God. The ultimate reward for these labors is to be as God is and to dwell in the celestial kingdom with God and Christ forever.

As with the prior Beatitudes, the Savior had ideals which would help the leaders of his kingdom achieve the goal of being sanctified or pure in heart. These items are in addition to receiving the necessary ordinances. Cross-references for "pure in heart" in the current edition of the scriptures refer the reader to verses regarding chastity. Therefore, it is appropriate that the first ideal for this Beatitude is to require an enhanced compliance with the law of chastity. Tied in with that concept are the ideals of avoiding evil and divorce. The last ideal discussed in this beatitude is the Savior's counsel about deceit in communications. Each will be discussed in the order presented by the Savior.

The Law of Chastity

The Savior began this ideal by quoting another law of Moses. He said,

> Ye have heard that it was said by them of old time, Thou shalt not commit adultery. (Matthew 5:27; see also 3 Nephi 12:27)

When Moses presented the sixth of the Ten Commandments received from God after fleeing Egypt, it was not to introduce but to reinforce the law of chastity. That commandment had been in effect since Adam and Eve. Sexual relations are to be reserved for appropriate expression within the sacred bonds of marriage and only with the covenant party. If a person ignores and breaks this law, he or she is defiled; they become unclean. Therefore, the Spirit of God leaves. The scriptures also record that "whoso committeth adultery with a woman lacketh understanding: he that doeth it destroyeth his own soul" (Proverbs 6:32). In the hierarchy of sins, breaking the law of chastity is abominable before the Lord, "yea, most abominable above all sins save it be the shedding of innocent blood or denying the Holy Ghost" (Alma 39:5).

Beginning with Adam, those who were righteous or were pure in heart saw God in high places. After Moses was instrumental in releasing Israel from bondage in Egypt, the glory of God was associated with the tabernacle (see Numbers 9:15–22, Deuteronomy 31:15). Those who carried the components that comprised that sacred structure were required to be pure. Nor were any who were unclean allowed to touch the ark of the covenant. Those who did so and were impure were struck down. Many years later in the promised land, Solomon, king of Israel, was allowed to construct a temple at Jerusalem wherein was housed the ark and other sacred items to remind the tribes of Israel of God's mercy toward them. This sacred edifice was where all the sacrifices intended to direct Israel to Christ were performed. As with the tabernacle, those who were to enter the temple had to be pure. There was no exception made if one were to administer the rites or be the recipient. All had to be clean and pure.

Many hundreds of years before Christ, the prophet Isaiah encouraged all who entered sacred places to be clean. One reason was to prepare people to receive the Holy Ghost when they entered a dedicated structure (see Isaiah 52:11) for it is the Spirit which cleanses or purifies one of all sin. Those who are sinful cannot see God and live (see Exodus 33:20 JST). In the Americas, the prophet Nephi taught his people this principle when he said that nothing unclean could dwell with God (see 1 Nephi 10:21). With the renewed construction of temples in modern times, the admonition to remain pure is just as important now as it was then. The Lord told the Prophet Joseph Smith,

> And inasmuch as my people build a house unto me in the name of the Lord, and do not suffer any unclean thing to come into it, that it be not defiled, my glory shall rest upon it;
>
> Yea, and my presence shall be there, for I will come into it, and all the pure in heart that shall come into it shall see God.
>
> But if it be defiled I will not come into it, and my glory shall not be there; for I will not come into unholy temples. (Doctrine and Covenants 97:15–17)

Over the centuries the Lord, through his prophets, has equated obedience to the law of chastity with being clean or pure. As the Prophet Joseph Smith pointed out, God's presence is in the temples. The pure in heart who enter therein shall see God. But there is a warning. If the temple is defiled, God will not remain in an unholy place.

In modern revelations, the Lord has been very specific. Those who break the law of chastity and fail to repent are relegated to a lesser kingdom of glory. They will be servants of the Most High, but where God and Christ dwell, they cannot come (see Doctrine and Covenants 76:98–99, 103, 109–112).

But this requirement of being clean or pure is even more important for the leaders of Christ's Church. Besides being visible examples of the Savior's teachings, a leader who is guilty of sexual sin has rejected Christ and his teachings. They refuse their responsibilities to maintain the standards of Christ as is the duty of those called to leadership, and they lose the right to the Holy Ghost. The end result is that they break covenants freely entered and are no longer pure in heart.

As has been mentioned, those who are pure qualify to enter the temple of God where the exalting ordinances are performed. The promised result of being pure in heart is the opportunity of seeing God. It should be noted that exaltation is essentially the same blessing as that of other Beatitudes. All of Christ's actions point toward helping his brothers and sisters achieve the celestial kingdom.

There is an extension to the concept of temples and the need to be pure. A temple is not restricted to a dedicated structure nor a mountaintop nor grove of trees. A temple is also a person's physical body. Paul taught this concept in an epistle to the Corinthians when he wrote,

> Know ye not that ye are the temple of God, and that spirit of God dwelleth in you?
>
> If any man defile the temple of God, him shall God destroy; for the temple of God is holy, which temple ye are. (1 Corinthians 3:16–17)

Paul didn't stop with this council. Within the same epistle, he repeated the concept and specified one area which would defile God's temple. This time he referred to the Mosaic law of foods which considered certain foods unclean and would defile the body.

> Meats for the belly, and the belly for meats: but God shall destroy both it and them. Now the body is not for fornication, but for the Lord; and the Lord is for the body. . . .
>
> Know ye not that your bodies are the members of Christ? Shall I then take the members of Christ, and make them the members of an harlot? God forbid.

> What? Know ye not that he which is joined to an harlot is one body? For two, saith he, shall be one flesh.
>
> But he that is joined unto the Lord is one spirit.
>
> Flee fornication. Every sin that a man doeth is without the body; but he that committeth fornication sinneth against his own body.
>
> What? Know ye not that your body is the temple of the Holy Ghost which is in you, which ye have of God, and ye are not your own?
>
> For ye are bought with a price; therefore glorify God in your body, and in your spirit, which are Gods. (1 Corinthians 6:13, 15–20)

As Paul has stated, we are bought with a price. Christ's atonement has made it possible for our sins to be forgiven and our lives cleansed. He made it possible for all mankind to be resurrected. Thus, our bodies are his; we are members of Christ, a temple of the Holy Ghost, and nothing should be done which would make it unclean. Sexual misconduct of all kinds are sins that defile God's temple, our body, and forfeit the blessing of being like and with Christ.

In the prior beatitude, "blessed are the peacemakers," Christ reiterated the law of Moses regarding murder as a prelude for instructions to avoid anger. In this latest beatitude, Christ follows the same process. He had quoted the law given by Moses, which confirms the law of chastity and the sanctity of the marriage covenant. Then the Savior expands the disciple's vision of their responsibilities as leaders in his kingdom:

> But I say unto you, that whosoever looketh on a woman to lust after her hath committed adultery already in his heart. (Matthew 5:28; see also 3 Nephi 12:28)

Leaders who follow the higher law are expected to avoid lustful thoughts or anything like unto it. Elder Spencer W. Kimball helped explain this concept to the Saints when he said that

> home breaking is sin, and any thought, act or association which will tend to destroy another's home is a grievous transgression. (*Conference Report*, October 1962, p. 58)

Elder Bruce R. McConkie wrote,

> There are no grosser personal crimes than adultery, except murder and the commission of the unpardonable sin (Alma 59:5–6). Adulterous acts are committed mentally before the physical debauchery ever takes place, and sensual and evil thoughts are in themselves a debasing evil. (*Mormon Doctrine*, p. 23–24, 638–639)

Ancient scriptures and modern prophets stress that adultery is a grievous transgression. But the warning doesn't stop there. This or any other sin is conceived and committed mentally prior to the actual event taking place. Therefore, our thoughts are to be controlled. After the Restoration of God's kingdom in latter days had begun, the Lord reiterated this principle to Joseph Smith:

> And verily I say unto you, as I have said before, he that looketh on a woman to lust after her, or if any shall commit adultery in their hearts, they shall not have the Spirit, but shall deny the faith and shall fear. (Doctrine and Covenants 63:16)

The Lord's instructions are clear: those who commit adultery or even look upon a person with lust will lose their connection with the Spirit. If individuals do not repent and correct their lives, they will suffer the second death—not being in Christ's presence and not participating in the First Resurrection (see Doctrine and Covenants 63:17–18). Thus, they shall not see God.

Later in his ministry the Savior taught that

> those things which proceed out of the mouth come forth from the heart; and they defile the man.
>
> For out of the heart proceed evil thoughts, murders, adulteries, fornication, thefts, false witness, blasphemies:
>
> These are the things which defile a man. (Matthew 15:18–20)

In an address given in the April 1962 General Conference, the prophet of that time, President David O. McKay, outlined a process of how eternal destinies grow from thoughts. He said,

> Sow a thought, reap an act,
> Sow an act, reap a habit,
> Sow a habit, reap a character,
> Sow a character, reap an eternal destiny."
> (Quoting E. D. Boardman in *Conference Report*, April 1962, p. 7)

Thus, as was spoken of by the Savior and through the process mentioned by President McKay, a thought can influence our eternal destiny. If an individual keeps thoughts pure, a celestial destiny is received, but if thoughts are allowed to be unclean, lesser destinies must be expected.

God's house is one of order, not of confusion (see Doctrine and Covenants 132:8; 1 Corinthians 14:33). In order to enter the highest degree of the celestial kingdom, where God dwells and to be as he is, an individual must be married in a temple by one duly authorized (see

Doctrine and Covenants 131:1–4). The promise shown in the scriptures is that if all the requirements are met, the individual will not just see God but will be as God (see Doctrine and Covenants 132:19–20).

This great blessing cannot come to pass if an individual succumbs to the temptations of Lucifer and fails to repent. The adversary's greatest and perhaps most effective tool in breaking up a potential celestial family unit is sexual sin. This sin destroys trust and love between a husband and wife while preventing God's Spirit from providing needed guidance. Thus, a disciple of Christ, especially a leader in Christ's Church, must avoid that which would destroy a family unit. But a leader must be even more cautious than those in his or her stewardship. A leader must guard even against inappropriate thoughts.

In the modern world of television, VCRs, DVDs, and the internet, extra caution is warranted. Inappropriate situations are portrayed in the media as acceptable, and those who disapprove of that material are considered out of step, outdated, or grossly ignorant. Language in music and books is another avenue by which Satan's pernicious message is spread. Then the internet is used by evil and conspiring men to make pornography accessible to an ever-wider and younger audience. President Spencer W. Kimball warned the modern Saints to avoid that which creates obscene thoughts as he or she would shun an enemy. He said,

> The stench of obscenity and vulgarity reaches and offends the heavens. It putrefies all it touches.
>
> Each person must keep himself clean and free from lusts. He must shun ugly, polluted thoughts and acts as he would an enemy. Pornography and erotic stories and pictures are worse than polluted food. Shun these. The body has power to rid itself of sickening food. That person who

entertains filthy stories or pornographic pictures and literature records these in his marvelous human computer, the brain, which can't forget this filth. Once recorded, it will always remain there, subject to recall—filthy images. (*The Teachings of Spencer W. Kimball*, p. 282–283)

The conclusion is that all of these carnal practices are used by Lucifer to degrade an individual in a gradual process until even the most heinous acts seem acceptable. From that point, Satan works to encircle the individual with his chains and drag him or her down to hell (see Alma 12:10–12).

An example of this progression to destruction is shown in the life of David, king of Israel. During his youth, David had sufficient faith in the God of Israel to face and defeat Goliath. Years later, after being anointed king, he was able to build Israel into a regional power. But then David saw Bathsheba and harbored illicit desires. As mentioned by President McKay, the progression eventually went from a thought to an action. It is not known how long this process took, but Bathsheba and David committed adultery. Then, to cover the sin, Bathsheba's husband, Uriah, was killed (see 2 Samuel 11). Rather than being concealed, the sin was revealed and David lost his exaltation (see Doctrine and Covenants 132:39).

A leader in Christ's Church must live the law of chastity, as do all that desire to live with and be as God. In this training, the Savior instructs his disciples to even avoid lustful thoughts. Those who fail in this, who have sinful thoughts and do not repent, will lose the Spirit. Without the protection of the Spirit of God, the individual will eventually deny the faith and lose their opportunity for exaltation. The leaders who are diligent in avoiding these temptations and keep themselves pure will not only see God but will live with him.

Avoid Evil

The next topic the disciples had to be aware of to keep their lives pure was that of avoiding evil. This may seem a simplistic and common-sense approach, but all too often we, as a people, flirt with the devil and expect to walk with angels. The Savior wanted the leaders of his kingdom to avoid this misconception when he said,

> If thy right eye offend thee, pluck it out, and cast it from thee: for it is profitable for thee that one of thy members should perish, and not that thy whole body should be cast into hell.
>
> And if thy right hand offend thee, cut it off, and cast it from thee: for it is profitable for thee that one of thy members should perish, and not that thy whole body should be cast into hell. And now this I speak, a parable concerning your sins; wherefore, cast them from you, that ye may not be hewn down and cast into the fire. (Matthew 5:29–30 JST)

In order to survive or prosper during the meridian of time, an individual needed a sound body. If a limb were lost, then the planting couldn't be done, crops couldn't be harvested, flocks couldn't be cared for, or products couldn't be made. For that reason, a limb was taken only if life was threatened. There were no agencies of a government responsible to assist the disabled or handicapped. Nor were there private organizations to provide assistance. Those individuals who were impaired were dependent on the mercy of those passing by to provide sustenance for themselves and their family.

The gist of these instructions is that instead of removing an eye or having a limb amputated to save lives, the disciples were to eliminate sins, inappropriate actions, or bad habits from their lives to save their souls. Anything that would hinder God's Spirit from being present or make an individual unclean must be avoided or cut out.

Elder Bruce R. McConkie in his *Doctrinal New Testament Commentary* (DNTC) offered this explanation:

> In a figurative manner of speaking various organs of the body are said to commit sin when what is actually meant is that the person himself is guilty of the evil deed. We refer to someone as having a lying *tongue,* meaning he is a liar. We speak of "*hands* that shed innocent blood," *hearts* that devise "wicked imaginations, *feet* that be swift in running to mischief." (Proverbs 6:16–18), *eyes* guilty of lust (1 John 2:16), and so forth. And this is the type and kind of expression used by Jesus in his parable about destroying offending members of the body as a means of casting one's sins away.
>
> If thy right eye offend thee, pluck it out and cast it from thee – that is, if a situation or circumstance exists which might lead to sin, avoid it, but continued association therewith leads to sin. If thy neighbor's wife is unduly attractive to you, stay away from her. If you have an urge to gamble, don't associate with gamblers or go where gambling is found. If you love money and the riches of men, consecrate your properties to the Welfare Plan and ask your bishop to recommend you for a mission (Matthew 19:16–26). If you have an urge to steal, lock yourself in your closet until it passes. If the smell of coffee is enticing, don't go where it is being prepared.
>
> If thy right hand offend thee, cut it off and cast it from thee – that is, get away from the environment of sin. Forsake

the world, including father and mother, brothers and sisters, if need be. Do not let evil thoughts enter your mind, lest they become your master. Live a life of severe spiritual discipline. If it is more difficult for you to keep the commandments than it is for your neighbor, avoid the enticements which have no pulling power on him. (DNTC 1:224–225)

In addition to avoiding situations or circumstances that might lead to sin, Elder McConkie mentioned forsaking family if they would lead an individual to evil. President Joseph Fielding Smith referred to the passages of the Sermon on the Mount quoted earlier and said,

> When the Lord spoke of parts of the body it is evident that he had in mind close friends or relatives who endeavored to lead us from the paths of rectitude and humble obedience to the divine commandments we receive from the Lord.
>
> If any friend or relative endeavors to lead a person away from the commandments, it is better to dispense with his friendship and association rather than to follow him in evil practices to destruction. This use of comparison or illustration was as common in ancient days as it is in the present age. We should not, in reading these ancient expressions in the New Testament, take such a statement as this referred to in the words of the Savior recorded by Mark in the literal interpretation. When properly understood it becomes a very impressive figure of speech. (Answers to Gospel Questions 5:79)

In these two verses, Christ instructed the leaders of his Church in Palestine to cast all that is evil from their lives. This was not limited to practices or a way of life but included any individual that might lead one from the path God has designated. Families were not granted an exemption.

This idea applies to all of God's children, but for leaders in Christ's Church, it takes on added meaning. In an earlier beatitude, the Savior charged his disciples with the responsibility of keeping the doctrines and ordinances of the kingdom in their pure form. But there have been, are, and will continue to be people who persist in teaching false doctrines or desire to alter the exalting ordinances. If an individual continues to publicly teach error and refuses to repent when so counseled by his or her leaders, the person must be removed from membership in the kingdom. It is better that a member of Christ's Church be removed than the whole destroyed.

After Christ had ascended into heaven and Peter became the Chief Apostle for those in Palestine, the Saints were attempting to live the law of consecration. Ananias and his wife, Sapphira, tried to present the appearance of righteousness—to live the letter of the law rather than its spirit. They withheld a portion of their property and represented that all their goods had been consecrated for the benefit of the kingdom. The Spirit testified to Peter of their duplicity and the Lord struck the couple down. Rather than let his fledgling Church become tainted, God removed the corrupting influence (see Acts 5:1–10).

The Saints in the New World had their own teachers of false doctrine. These teachers of error were cast out rather than allowed to destroy or corrupt God's children. The scriptures record that the people of Ammon cast Nehor out. This false prophet was then brought before Alma, the high priest, and rebuked.

The admonition to remove the unrepentant from the rolls of the Church remains in force in the modern organization. The Lord told the Prophet Joseph Smith,

> He that receiveth my law and doeth it, the same is my disciple; and he that saith he receiveth it not, the same is not my disciple, and shall be cast out from among you. (Doctrine and Covenants 41:5)

Christ commands that those who espouse or teach apostate doctrines or commit grievous sins be removed from the Church if they do not repent. The guilty lose the blessings of their baptism, the companionship of the Holy Ghost, the priesthood (if male and ordained), as well as any temple ordinances that have been received. Due to the serious nature of this action, the Lord has provided a procedure for leaders to follow (see Doctrine and Covenants 102:13–24). The intent and desire of this process is to protect the Church, preserve the innocent, and help the guilty repent.

The concept of avoiding evil was also taught to the disciples in the New World. But in that version of this leadership training, the Savior used different words to accommodate a different people. He said,

> Behold, I give unto you a commandment, that ye suffer none of these things to enter into your heart;
>
> For it is better that ye should deny yourselves of these things, wherein ye will take up your cross, than that ye should be cast into hell. (3 Nephi 12:29–30)

Just as in Palestine, the Savior instructed his American disciples to avoid adultery and lust. Then he added that the leaders in his kingdom were not to allow anything into their hearts that might lead to sin. It is better that they deny themselves of the concepts of the world than to be cast into hell. They are to take up their cross as Christ. The Savior completed the Atonement and made the Resurrection possible by dying on the cross. He gave up his life for his disciples and mankind. Thus, to be pure in heart, one must take up the cross, which means to give up all the actions, habits, and thoughts that lead away from Christ and the kingdom of God.

Divorce

As was mentioned in the discussion regarding the law of chastity, an individual must be married in the temple of God by those in authority to enter the celestial kingdom. This ordinance marks the creation of a unit necessary for a couple to become as God is. Therefore, marriage is something that should not be entered into on a whim nor ended for specious reasons. The Savior told the Apostles in Palestine,

> It hath been said, Whosoever shall put away his wife, let him give her a writing of divorcement:
>
> But I say unto you, that whosoever shall put away his wife, saving for the cause of fornication, causeth her to commit adultery: and whosoever shall marry her that is divorced committeth adultery. (Matthew 5:31–32; see also 3 Nephi 12:31–32)

In these verses, Christ follows the procedure established earlier: the Lord quotes or refers to the law of Moses (see Deuteronomy 24:1) or practices based on that law; then, to assist his disciples in their effort to be pure in heart, the Savior expands or gives further depth to this concept. With these teachings, he can stress once again the sanctity of both the law of chastity and the ordinance of marriage.

At the time these instructions were given, the practice or procedure regarding the obtaining of divorces had become very lax in both portions of the world. A husband could obtain a divorce from his wife for any or no reason; much like the laws and practices that are followed today. This practice devalues marriage from a sacred ordinance to an event similar to the purchase of a commodity. If the item isn't satisfactory, simply return the product with a receipt for a full refund. A receipt isn't even necessary to end a marriage—just a nebulous excuse that "things didn't work out." Christ's teachings came in opposition to the practice of his day. He taught that once entered, a marriage covenant could only be broken by the infidelity of either the husband or the wife.

Late in his Palestinian ministry, while teaching in Judea, the Savior was surrounded by many people. Included in the crowds were Pharisees. Their intent was not to listen to the Savior to learn of God's kingdom but rather to find a way to fault Christ and maintain their status. Matthew recorded a confrontation with these Pharisees and the teaching that resulted:

> The Pharisees also came unto him, tempting him, and saying unto him, Is it lawful for a man to put away his wife for every cause?
>
> And he answered and said unto them, Have ye not read, that he which made them at the beginning made them male and female,
>
> And said, for this cause shall a man leave father and mother, and shall cleave to his wife: and they twain shall be one flesh?
>
> Wherefore they are no more twain, but one flesh. What therefore God hath joined together, let not man put asunder. (Matthew 19:3–6)

When the Pharisees asked about divorce, the Savior responded by reaffirming the sacred nature of marriage. It was God's original intent that when a man and woman wed, they were to become one in purpose: to be one flesh and become a unit that could be as God. Once marriage has joined two people, they should not allow anything to disturb their union. Hence the counsel to "let not man put asunder what God hath joined together."

The Pharisees could not or would not accept this counsel because it went counter to their actions.

> They say unto him, Why did Moses then command to give a writing of divorcement, and to put her away?
>
> He saith unto them, Moses because of the hardness of your hearts suffered you to put away your wives: but from the beginning it was not so.
>
> And I say unto you, Whosoever shall put away his wife, except it be for fornication, and shall marry another, committeth adultery: and whoso marrieth her which is put away doth commit adultery. (Matthew 19:7–9)

The Pharisees tried to use Moses to justify their actions and evade the subtle rebuke which had been given, but Christ stopped them. The Savior reminded those who should have known better that when marriage was instituted, divorce had never been intended. It is pride and sin that requires the need for a process that breaks up a godly unit. Thus, in God's eyes, the only justifiable reason for a divorce was infidelity to marriage vows. Elder James Talmage wrote,

> Jesus declared that except for the most serious offense of infidelity to marriage vows, no man could divorce his wife without becoming himself an offender, in that she, marrying again while still a wife not righteously divorced, would be

guilty of sin, and so would be the man to whom she was so married. (*Jesus the Christ*, p. 234–235)

Also writing on the subject Elder Bruce R. McConkie taught,

> Under the law of Moses, divorce came easily; but recently freed from Egyptian slavery, the chosen race had yet to attain the social, cultural, and spiritual stability that exalts marriage to its proper place in the eternal scheme of things. Men were empowered to divorce their wives for any unseemly thing. It hath been said, Whosoever shall put away his wife, let him give her a writing of divorcement.
>
> No such low and base standard is acceptable under gospel law. Thus Jesus summarized his perfect marriage order by saying: 'But I say unto you, That whosoever shall put away his wife, saving for the cause of fornication, causeth her to commit adultery: and whosoever shall marry her that is divorced committeth adultery.' Divorce is totally foreign to celestial standards, a verity that Jesus will one day expound in more detail to the people of Jewry. For now, as far as the record reveals, he merely specifies the high law that his people should live, but that is beyond our capability even today. If husbands and wives, lived the law as the Lord would have them live it, they would neither do or say the things that would even permit the fleeting thought of divorce to enter the mind of their eternal companions. Though we today have the gospel, we have yet to grow into that high state of marital association where marrying a divorced person constitutes adultery. The Lord has not yet given us the high standard he here named as that which ultimately will replace the

Mosaic practice of writing a bill of divorcement. (*The Mortal Messiah* 2:138–139)

The law for the leaders of Christ's Church today is simple: "Husbands and wives are to live so that they would neither do nor say the things that would permit the thought of divorce to enter the mind of their eternal companion." In this they would be pure in heart.

Deceit/Oaths

All too often people use words in a manner that is perceived in one way by the audience but disguises the real intent of an individual. There is any number of reasons for this behavior. A politician desires to be elected or remain in office and desires not to alienate voters. Companies seek to encourage people to purchase goods and services. Still others seek to avoid criticism or offense by being misleading. In large measure, the intent behind this method of communication is to mislead the audience. When the audience observes actions or decisions of that person that do not match the statements the speaker points to, their statements and proclaims innocence. Obvious consequences follow: voters come to distrust their elected leaders; the public questions the claims of a company; a person wonders if their neighbor is telling the truth. The next ideal taught by the Savior instructs the leaders of his kingdom to be forthright and truthful and to conduct their lives without verbal gymnastics. Christ said,

> Again, ye have heard that it hath been said by them of old time, Thou shalt not forswear thyself, but shalt perform unto the Lord thine oaths.
>
> But I say unto you, Swear not at all; neither by heaven; for it is God's throne:

Nor by the earth; for it is his footstool: neither by Jerusalem; for it is the city of the great king.

Neither shalt thou swear by thy head, because thou canst not make one hair white or black.

But let your communication be, Yea, yea; Nay, nay: for whatsoever is more than these cometh of evil" (Matthew 5:33–37)

The instructions given to the American disciples are essentially the same with the exception of the last verse. At the temple in the land Bountiful, Christ said, "But let your communications be Yea, yea; Nay, nay: for whatsoever cometh more than these is evil" (3 Nephi 12:37). The difference from the wording in the Book of Mormon enhances the understanding of Christ's message. Misleading people does not come from evil; it is evil.

In the meridian of time, an individual would lend credence to their message or give strength to their argument by swearing an oath. The items they would swear by were designed to add strength and credibility to the message. If an individual swore by Jerusalem, the listeners could be reasonably sure what was said was true. If the earth or other items evidenced the message, there was more room for doubt. For an item to be accepted as the complete truth, the oath would be sealed by the most sacred items in Jewish life: the temple, the altars, and the ark of the covenant. Although this hierarchy of oaths was in place, it was misused and abused. It became difficult to know when someone was telling the truth and would fulfill their promises or when someone was intending to deceive.

For a leader to be pure in heart, he or she cannot teach or conduct his or her life with the intent to deceive. If the kingdom of God is to progress, it is paramount that the leaders of Christ's Church be understood, believed, and trusted and that their counsel be followed. Thus, Christ taught his disciples and Apostles to avoid the use of oaths as evidence to the truth of their statement in all aspects of life. They were to speak plainly, without guile or intent to deceive. This counsel is extended beyond gospel truths to all facets of life so the Saints would not err (see 2 Nephi 25:20).

An ideal taught in an earlier beatitude by Christ stressed that it is very important for a leader to be an example of righteousness. This requirement cannot be met if a leader's statements must be parsed in an effort to discover whether or not the real meaning agrees with the perceived meaning. The Apostle Paul in his second epistle to the Corinthians instructed the Saints of his time that the gospel taught by Christ was even more glorious than the law of Moses. He said, "Seeing thou that we have such hope, we use great plainness of speech" (see 2 Corinthians 3:12).

James wrote to the twelve tribes of Israel this same council:

> But above all things, my brethren, swear not, neither by heaven, neither by the earth, neither by any other oath: but let your yea be yea; and your nay, nay; lest ye fall into condemnation. (James 5:12)

Nephi, an American prophet who lived hundreds of years before Christ, also taught in plainness. He said,

> For my soul delighteth in plainness; for after this manner doth the Lord God work among the children of men. For the Lord God giveth light unto the understanding: for he speaketh unto men according to their language, unto their understanding. (2 Nephi 31:3)

This great prophet taught his people in plainness. It was not because he was unsophisticated or uneducated but because he followed the Saviors instructions. He taught with plain speech, in the language of his listeners, as an aid to understanding.

With the Restoration of the gospel, the Lord told the Prophet Joseph Smith,

> And for this cause, that men might be made partakers of the glories which were to be revealed, the Lord sent forth the fullness of his gospel, his everlasting covenant, reasoning in plainness and simplicity. (Doctrine and Covenants 133:57)

As mentioned earlier, the purpose of the gospel and Christ's Church is to give God's children the opportunity to receive the necessary doctrines and ordinances to be exalted. These teachings are not to be couched in secrecy or in complexity. It is intended that all understand the doctrines and requirements which must be met to receive this wonderful blessing. Thus, it is to be taught plainly, in simplicity, keeping with God's purpose.

Another area of speech that is harmful is flattery. This form of speech uses excessive praise, flowery phrases, and insincere acts to ingratiate one's self into another's confidence. "It includes the raising of false hopes; there is always an element of dishonesty attending it" (see *Mormon Doctrine*, p. 287). Thus, "a flattering mouth worketh ruin" (see Proverbs 26:28). The Prophet Joseph Smith said, "Flattery is . . . a deadly poison" (see *Teachings of the Prophet Joseph Smith*, p. 137).

Besides stirring people to anger against good and lulling them into carnal security, Lucifer uses flattery to drive a wedge in God's kingdom. The prophet Nephi taught,

> And behold, others he flattereth away, and telleth them there is no hell; and he saith unto them: I am no devil, for there is none—and thus he whispereth in their ears, until he grasps them with his awful chains, from whence there is no deliverance. (2 Nephi 28:22)

Flattery is used to reinforce what the people want to hear, and it is often detrimental to their spiritual wellbeing. In the verse just quoted, Nephi taught that the people would desire to be told there was no hell or devil. By association, the message would be that with no devil there was no sin. There would be no eternal consequences for any action or thought. Thus, Lucifer would grasp his victims with his "awful chains from whence there is no deliverance."

Examples of how this form of speech is harmful can be found in the reigns of King Noah and King Mosiah in the Book of Mormon. In one example, it was the leaders who used flattery to enhance their lifestyle. In the other, dissenters from the kingdom used flattery to lead others astray, and Christ's servants had to overcome the difficulty imposed.

King Noah and his priests were prideful and desired a life of leisure. To pay for what their leaders desired, onerous taxes were placed upon the people of Noah. But this is not all. Following the wicked example of their leaders the people also became idolatrous:

> Because they were deceived by the vain and flattering words of the king and priests: for they did speak flattering things unto them. (Mosiah 11:7)

Through the use of flattery, King Noah and his priests were able to convince their people there was no hell or devil and encouraged wickedness. The result of this was the death of many of the people of Noah at the hands of the Lamanites and the bondage of the survivors. Once again, "a flattering mouth worketh ruin."

The second example involves political dissent. Among the Nephites, there were those who dissented from the truth and the government. Over a period of time, these dissenters grew to be more numerous than the faithful.

> For it came to pass that they did deceive many with their flattering words, who were in the church, and did cause them to commit many sins; therefore it became expedient that those who committeth sin, that were in the church, should be admonished by the church. (Mosiah 26:6)

In both of the examples cited above, flattery was used to draw many away from the truth. Lives were disrupted; some ended. Sins were committed, and unhappiness resulted. Flattery has led to the downfall of many and requires the efforts of many to overcome. A leader in God's kingdom should not be guilty of using any method of communication "that has an element of dishonesty."

The next area of communications that is to be considered is gossip. Elder Bruce R. McConkie in his book *Mormon Doctrine* wrote,

> Gossip ordinarily consists in talebearing, in spreading scandal, in engaging in familiar or idle conversation dealing personally with other people's affairs. Frequently the reports are false; almost always they are so exaggerated and twisted as to give an unfair perspective, and in nearly every case they redound to the discredit of the person under consideration. It follows that gossip is unwholesome, serves no beneficial purpose, and should be shunned. (*Mormon Doctrine*, p. 336–337).

A leader must be careful in what he or she says. The Savior said, "That every idle word that men shall speak, they shall give an account thereof in the day of judgment" (see Matthew 12:36). Paul in his epistle to the Ephesians wrote,

> Let no corrupt communication proceed out of your mouth, but that which is good to the use of edifying, that it may minister grace unto the hearers. (Ephesians 4:29)

During a priesthood interview or while in council meetings, confidential information is provided which involves the lives of members of the Church. If a leader were to make this material public knowledge, lives would be disrupted. It may even have eternal consequences. The effects of disclosure of privileged information go beyond the original individual. As the source of the gossip becomes known, confidence is lost in the leader who spoke out of turn. Those in his or her stewardship may question the counsel or teachings given. They may refuse to provide necessary information in future meetings for fear it also will be disclosed as gossip.

The Lord has instructed his people, his leaders in particular, to deal in plain speech "for whatsoever cometh of more than this is evil." Gospel teachings should be to edify and exalt all. But more than this, all actions and speech should be without reproach and without guile. One cannot be pure in heart and work to deceive or manipulate their brothers and sisters. All communications must be truthful and straightforward.

Summary

Throughout the ages, the followers of Christ have been directed toward sacred places. It is in these sacred areas that prophets have seen visions, received instructions, or seen the Savior. It is in these sacred areas that the Saints receive power and enlightenment from on high. Before Moses, these holy places were found on the tops of certain high mountains. After the Lord used Moses to free Israel from bondage in Egypt, a tabernacle was erected to contain the sacred relics. Later, Solomon constructed a temple in Jerusalem wherein sacred ordinances were conducted. Prophets have also taught that our physical bodies are considered temples of the Holy Ghost.

Regardless of the location, altitude, or form, an individual must conform to the Lord's code of behavior to enter a holy place. By obedience, a person becomes clean or pure. During his efforts to call the people of Ammonihah to repentance, the prophet Alma said,

> Now they, after being sanctified by the Holy Ghost, having their garments made white, being pure and spotless before God, could not look upon sin save it were with abhorrence; and there were many, exceedingly great many, who were made pure and entered into the rest of the Lord their God. (Alma 13:12)

As part of the Sermon to teach his disciples leadership skills, the Savior outlined ideals for being pure in heart. Following a pattern established in prior Beatitudes, he discussed the Mosaic laws regarding adultery, divorce, and oaths, then provided a higher law.

The last ideal taught for being pure in heart is the concept of being honest or truthful in speech: "Every man's every word was to be as true and accurate as if it had been spoken with an oath" (DNTC 1:226). Flattery, gossip, saying anything misleading, or having the desire for deception are to be avoided. As many of the prophets of old, leaders are to use "plainness and simplicity in speech." The objective is not to confuse the people but to encourage all to come unto Christ.

Prior to that ideal, Christ turned to another aspect of the law of chastity which also has vast eternal consequences: divorce. Although divorce was allowed under the laws of Moses, the Savior taught that it is not appropriate for a person and, especially, for a leader to obtain a divorce from his or her eternal mate for any cause other than fornication. A leader is to cleave to his or her eternal mate and to act and speak so that the thought of divorce never comes.

Another ideal taught is that a leader must be rid of anything that is not in accordance with God's law or will. This includes but is not limited to habits or practices. People who strive against the gospel and who seek to prevent the exaltation of God's children are also to be avoided. This includes family. It is not possible for an individual to associate with people who are enemies to God or to engage in practices that are contrary to God's will and retain the Spirit of the Lord. It is the Spirit, which is a sanctifier and purifier.

The first ideal discussed for this beatitude was the law of chastity and its extension. When a couple is married in a temple by one holding the proper authority, a godly unit is established. If the couple continues in righteousness, they will become as our Heavenly Parents and continue the cycle of exaltation. Disobedience to the law of chastity threatens this sacred unit. While it is important for an individual to be clean from the sin of adultery, a leader must do more. He or she must learn to control their thoughts. A sin as grievous as adultery may end with the actual act, but it begins with a thought.

If a leader in Christ's Church strives to be pure in heart by obeying these instructions, they will qualify to stand with God and Christ. King David in a psalm wrote,

> Who shall ascend into the hill of the Lord? Or who shall stand in his holy place?

He that hath clean hands, and a pure heart; who hath not lifted up his soul unto vanity, nor sworn deceitfully.

He shall receive the blessing from the Lord, and righteousness from the God of his salvation. (Psalms 24:3–5)

BLESSED ARE THE MERCIFUL

Blessed are the merciful; for they shall obtain mercy. (Matthew 5:7; see also 3 Nephi 12:19)

"Blessed are the merciful" is the fifth beatitude introduced and the fourth explained. Often the injunction to be merciful is interpreted and applied in the context of an incorrect definition. To prevent a misunderstanding and misapplication of this principle, it is important to understand the Savior's intent. Outside of religious settings, mercy is defined as "refraining from harming or punishing offenders, enemies, persons in one's power, etc.; kindness in excess of what may be expected or demanded by fairness; forbearance and compassion" (*Webster's New World Dictionary*, Third College Edition, p. 849). With this definition, mercy may be granted to the deserving and undeserving alike. It is often applied in a capricious or arbitrary manner. Thus, an unrepentant serial murderer can be set free in application of mercy while a remorseful one-time shoplifter is required to live out the full extent of the prescribed sentence. There are no requirements set to receive this mercy.

"In the gospel sense, 'mercy' consists in our Lord's forbearance on certain specified conditions, from imposing punishments that, except for his grace and goodness, would be the just reward of man" (*Mormon Doctrine*, p. 483). Elder McConkie continues his explanation and writes that

> mercy is a gift the Lord reserves for his saints and their weaknesses (D&C 38:14; 50:16; 64:4); it is reserved for the meek, they who are the god-fearing and the righteous (D&C 97:2); because of it, they will be remembered in the day of wrath (D&C 101:9). Because of mercy men are enabled to repent (D&C 3:10); and when the elders of Israel "confess their sins with humble hearts," a merciful God forgives them of those sins (D&C 61:2). Indeed the Lords people may well ask themselves, "what doth the Lord require of thee, but to do justly, and to love mercy, and to walk humbly with thy God?" (Mic 6:8). (*Mormon Doctrine*, p. 484)

Mercy is a gift from God that is made possible by the Savior's Atonement. Those who repent of their sins and obey the commandments receive a remission of their sins. They can escape the eternal penalties associated with those sins while those who are disobedient and fail to repent endure full punishment. Prior to beginning their conquest of the promised land, the people of Israel were told,

> Know therefore that the Lord thy God, he is God, the faithful God, which keepeth covenant and mercy with them that love him and keep his commandments to a thousand generations;
>
> And repayeth them that hate him to their face, to destroy them: he will not be slack to him that hateth him, he will repay him to his face. (Deuteronomy 7:9–10)

For mercy to be granted or, in other words, for sins to be remitted, an individual must repent of those sins and be obedient to the commandments. President Brigham Young gave this concept a human face when he said,

> The merciful man shall find mercy. When a man designedly does wrong, he ought to be chastised for that wrong, receiving according to his works. If a man does wrong through ignorance, and manifests sincere sorrow for the wrong, he is the one whom we should forgive seventy times in a day if necessary, and not the one who has designedly done wrong and repents not. (*Discourses of Brigham Young*, p. 273)

President Spencer W. Kimball, a latter-day prophet, echoed President Young's concept over a hundred years later. In his instructions to the Saints of his day, he mentioned the interplay between justice and mercy.

> The Lord's program is unchangeable. His laws are immutable. They are not modified. Your opinions or mine do not make any difference and do not alter the laws. Many of the world think that eventually the Lord will be merciful and give to them "unearned" blessings. Mercy cannot rob justice. College professors will not give you a doctorate degree for a few weeks of cursory work in the university, nor can the Lord be merciful at the expense of justice. In this program, which is infinitely greater, we will each receive what we merit. (*Teachings of Spencer W. Kimball*, p. 150).

In the secular world, a person can receive "unearned" blessings through the misapplication of mercy. That will not happen in God's plan of exaltation (*the plan for God's children to return to be with God*).

The Savior is known for providing justice as well as granting mercy. But he makes clear that mercy will not rob justice, and in order for mercy to take precedence over justice, certain requirements must be met. On the American continent, the prophet Alma taught his wayward son, Corianton, about the relationship between mercy and justice. He taught that

> there is a law given, and a punishment affixed, and a repentance granted; which repentance, mercy claimeth; otherwise, justice claimed the creature and executed the law, and the law inflicted the punishment; if not so, the works of justice would be destroyed, and God cease to be God.
>
> But God ceaseth not to be God, and mercy claimeth the penitent, and mercy cometh because of the atonement; and the atonement bringeth to pass the resurrection of the dead; and the resurrection of the dead bringeth back men into the presence of God; and thus they are restored into his presence, to be judged according to their works, according to the law and justice.
>
> For behold, justice exerciseth all his demands, and also mercy claimeth all which is her own; and thus, none but the truly penitent are saved.
>
> What, do ye suppose that mercy can rob justice? I say unto you, Nay; not one whit. If so, God would cease to be God. (Alma 42:22–25)

Alma reminded his son that there are laws given by God. With those laws come blessings if obeyed and punishments if disobeyed (see Doctrine and Covenants 130:20–21). Those who break God's laws are subject to justice; they are to receive the eternal punishments that have been designated for the commandment which was broken. But if a law is broken and repentance occurs, mercy is applied. Christ's Atonement allows the penitent to have their sins remitted, to escape the punishment for the sin, and to remain in the presence of God rather than to be cast out.

The Prophet Joseph Smith in the second lecture on faith taught that "three things are necessary in order that any rational and intelligent being may exercise faith in God unto life and salvation. First, the idea that he actually exists. Secondly, a 'correct' idea of his character, perfections, and attributes. Thirdly, an actual knowledge that the course of life which he is pursuing is according to his will" (*Lectures on Faith*, p. 33). Then, in the third lecture, the prophet mentioned six items respecting the character of God. The second item listed is that God "is merciful and gracious, slow to anger, abundant in goodness, and that he was so from everlasting and will be to everlasting" (*Lectures on Faith*, p. 35).

In this beatitude, the Savior desired his disciples to be aware of this aspect of God's character. By knowing of God's mercy and its proper application, the leaders of Christ's Church can develop a stronger, active faith in Christ and extend mercy to others in the manner intended by the Savior. They can receive mercy in turn, have their sins remitted, and become more like their Father in Heaven. Joseph Smith taught that

> it is equally important that men should have the idea of the existence of the attribute mercy in the Deity, in order to exercise faith in him for life and salvation, for without the idea of the existence of this attribute in the Deity, the spirits of the saints would faint in the midst of the tribulations, afflictions, and persecutions which they have to endure for righteousness sake. But when the idea of the existence of

> this attribute is once established in the mind it gives life and energy to the spirits of the saints, believing that the mercy of God will be poured out upon them in the midst of their afflictions, and that he will be compassionate for them in their sufferings, and that the mercy of God will lay hold of them and secure them in the arms of his love, so that they will receive a full reward for all their sufferings. (*Lectures on Faith*, p. 44)

By having a correct knowledge of God's mercy, the leaders of Christ's Church continue to strengthen their faith, which enables them to endure the tribulations that will beset them as they fulfill their responsibilities. This knowledge will give life and energy in their mission.

Another aspect of this Beatitude is the requirement of being merciful to others in order to receive mercy from God. Later in his ministry, Christ gave a parable that exemplified this concept. He taught,

> Therefore is the kingdom of heaven likened unto a certain king, which would take account of his servants.
>
> And when he had begun to reckon, one was brought unto him, which owed him ten thousand talents.
>
> But forasmuch as he had not to pay, his lord commanded him to be sold, and his wife, and children, and all that he had, and payment to be made.
>
> The servant therefore fell down, and worshipped him, saying, Lord, have patience with me, and I will pay thee all.
>
> Then the Lord of that servant was moved with compassion, and loosed him, and forgave him the debt.
>
> But the same servant went out, and found one of his fellowservants, which owed him an hundred pence: and he laid

hands on him, and took him by the throat, saying, Pay me that thou owest.

And his fellowservant fell down at his feet, and besought him, saying, Have patience with me, and I will pay thee all.

And he would not: but went and cast him into prison, till he should pay the debt.

So when his fellowservants saw what was done, they were very sorry, and came and told unto their lord all that was done.

Then his lord, after that he had called him, said unto him, O thou wicked servant, I forgave thee all that debt, because thou desirest me:

Shouldst not thou also have had compassion on thy fellowservant, even as I had pity on thee?

And his lord was wroth, and delivered him to the tormentors, till he should pay all that was due unto him.

So likewise shall my heavenly Father do also unto you, if ye from your hearts forgive not every one his brother their trespasses. (Matthew 18:23–35)

The first servant owed his lord a huge debt. Some have portrayed this amount by comparing the sum owed to a million dollars. When called to account, the first servant cried for and received mercy. Yet that same servant who had been forgiven of a huge financial obligation cast another into jail for a dime (see DNTC, p. 430). When the lord learned of this behavior, the first servant was called before his master once again and condemned. This judgment was rendered not for defaulting on the debt but for the lack of mercy.

And so it is in the dealings of the Eternal King with his servants. Sooner or later all face an enforced rendering of accounts, all are subjected to temptation, trials, and impending death, and all are rewarded with mercy or justice as their situations merit. Mercy is for the merciful, justice, retribution and punishment fall upon those who have dealt harshly with their fellow servants. (DNTC, p. 428)

Thus, Christ taught his disciples to be merciful that they might receive mercy and thereby receive their exaltation. In his teaching the ideals for this beatitude, the Savior shows the leaders of his Church the necessary application of mercy which will bless the lives of God's children. His work of exalting his brothers and sisters will go forward. The ideals of mercy Church leaders are to concentrate on are retaliation, persecution by legal process, lending, and the law of love and perfection. The last ideal of perfection is also a summary for those Beatitudes previously presented.

Retaliation

> Ye have heard that it hath been said, An eye for an eye, and a tooth for a tooth:
>
> But I say unto you, That ye resist not evil: but whosoever shall smite thee on thy right cheek, turn to him the other also. (Matthew 5:38–39; see also 3 Nephi 12:38–39)

This is the last beatitude in the Sermon on the Mount where the Savior quotes a law of Moses in preparation for adding his teachings. The portion of the law of Moses Christ was referring to states,

> And he that killeth a beast shall make it good: beast for beast.
>
> And if a man cause a blemish in his neighbor; as he hath done, so shall it be done to him;

> Breach for breach, eye for eye, tooth for tooth: as he hath caused a blemish in a man, so shall it be done to him again. (Leviticus 24:18–20)

The law of Moses required that any individual who caused a loss of property, a blemish in another, or the loss of an eye or a limb would receive the same loss or injury. An individual who caused the loss of his neighbor's beast would be required to replace the animal. If an arm or leg was maimed due to the actions of another, the perpetrator would receive the same injury. The only avenue the perpetrator had to escape receiving an injury similar to the one he or she caused was to make reparations. A price in gold or silver could be paid to compensate for the loss of an eye or limb or any other defect. Thus, justice would be served.

In his teachings to his disciples, the Savior changed the law of retaliation. The leaders of Christ's Church were not to exact justice. They were to extend mercy. Luke the physician gave a reason for this when he recorded,

> And unto him who smiteth thee on the cheek, offer also the other; or, in other words, it is better to offer the other, than to revile again. And him who taketh away thy cloak, forbid not to take away thy coat also.
>
> For it is better that thou suffer thine enemy to take these things, than to contend with him. Verily I say unto you, Your heavenly Father who seeth in secret, shall bring that wicked one into judgment. (Luke 6:29–30 JST)

Elder James Talmage in *Jesus the Christ* wrote:

> Of old the principle of retaliation had been tolerated, by which one who had suffered an injury could exact or inflict

a penalty of the same nature as the offense. Thus an eye was demanded for the loss of an eye, a tooth for a tooth, a life for a life. (See Exo 21:23-25; Lev 24:17-22; Deut 19:21). In contrast, Christ taught that men should rather suffer than do evil even to the extent of submission without resistance under certain implied conditions. His forceful illustrations—that if one were smitten on one cheek he should turn the other to the smiter; that if a man took another's coat by process of law, the loser should allow his coat to be taken also; that if one was pressed into service to carry another's burden a mile, he should willingly go two miles; that one should readily give or lend as asked—are not be to construed as commanding abject subserviency to unjust demands, nor as an abrogation of the principle of self-protection. These instructions were directed primarily to the apostles who would be professedly devoted to the work of the Kingdom to the exclusion of all other interest. In their ministry it would be better to suffer material loss or personal indignity and imposition at the hands of wicked oppressors, than to bring about an impairment of efficiency and a hindrance in work through resistance and contention. (*Jesus the Christ*, p. 235-236)

In this ideal, Christ provides the example of having one's cheek slapped or struck. This act is an insult or brings indignity. The initial impulse is to retaliate—to provide injury for injury, indignity for indignity, all driven by pride. But the Savior requires that his leaders cast out pride and resist not indignities. Otherwise, the work of the kingdom would be stopped as leaders retaliated for each indignity received. As Talmage points out, the call of leadership in the kingdom is to further the progress of the kingdom. It is not to gratify the pride or vain ambitions of the leader (see Doctrine and Covenants 121:37).

Another aspect in this counsel is the desire to avoid contention. Bruce R. McConkie in his series about the Savior wrote that "retaliation—with the inevitable bitterness and smallness of soul that attends it—cannot do other than keep hatred alive in the souls of men. If a man gouge out the eye of his neighbor, what benefit accrues to the wounded person if he retaliate by gouging out the eye of the offender? Has he enlarged his own soul, or has he permitted it to shrivel to the same smallness as the soul of his attacker?" (*The Mortal Messiah* 2:140).

> Contention leads to bitterness and smallness of soul; persons who contend with each other shrivel up spiritually and are in danger of losing their salvation. So important is it to avoid this evil that Jesus expected his saints to suffer oppression and wrong rather than lose their inner peace and serenity through contention. "He that hath the spirit of contention is not of me," he told the Nephites, "but is of the devil, who is the father of contention, and he stirreth up the hearts of men to contend with anger, one with another" (3 Nephi 11:29). (DNTC 1:228)

In order to have the work of exalting the Saints continue the Savior instructed his disciples in both Palestine and the Americas to show mercy to those who would insult or heap indignities upon them. Then as now, Church leaders are to forgo pride and not retaliate. By doing so they could concentrate on helping the saints achieve exaltation rather than spending time and resources retaliating for insults or injuries. As Elder Talmage mentioned these instructions 'are not to be construed as commanding abject subserviency or abrogation of the principle of self-protection.' They do not refer to life threatening dangers but refer to those insults or indignities which are of little or no moment. Nor are they intended to stop the disciples from their assigned duties to keep the doctrines and ordinances of the Kingdom pure. By extending mercy and not retaliating contention is reduced and the work of the Kingdom continues.

Persecution by Law

The second ideal in being merciful is similar to that of the first. Both encourage the leadership in Christ's kingdom to avoid contention by extending mercy. In the first beatitude discussed, Christ explained that Church leaders would have to endure persecution for maintaining in their pure form the doctrines, commandments, and ordinances that exalt the children of God. This latest ideal discusses the possibility that a leader may be persecuted by those opposing the kingdom through the use or misuse of the legal system. Pride would have those so persecuted retaliate in like manner. Christ taught his leaders differently. He said,

> And if any man will sue thee at the law, and take away thy cloak, let him have thy cloke also.
> And whosoever shall compel thee to go a mile, go with him twain. (Matthew 5:40–41; see also 3 Nephi 12:40–41)

In the quote by James Talmage cited earlier (see Retaliation), it was pointed out that these instructions were directed to the leaders of Christ's Church on earth. Church leaders were not instructed to accede to unjust demands, to not resist the wicked, nor to fail in their responsibilities to preserve the Church, its doctrines, and its ordinances in purity. The intent for these instructions was to keep Church leaders focused on their work for the kingdom rather than on lawsuits designed to harass and distract.

Bruce McConkie in his Messiah series echoed this sentiment when he wrote that "nothing is so important as the spread of truth and establishment of the cause of righteousness. The petty legal processes of that day must not be permitted to impede the setup up of the new Kingdom" (see *The Mortal Messiah* 2:141).

Rather than be contentious and dispute every wrong experienced, the leaders of Christ's kingdom are expected to be merciful. When frivolous or harassing lawsuits are brought against the Church and its leaders, the matter is to be resolved quickly so the work of salvation and exaltation can continue. This ties in with the earlier beatitude of being a peacemaker. Leaders are told to agree with their adversaries early to prevent lawsuits (refer to Compromise in the section "Blessed are the Peacemakers").

A modern example of this principle involved the purchase of a one-block segment of Main Street in Salt Lake City, Utah, by the Church. Millions of dollars were paid to the city for the land and millions more were spent to transform an asphalt road into a peaceful setting. The purpose for this effort was to provide a place where people could go to meditate or find a refuge from the concerns of daily life. The standards of the Church were to be observed, and protests or demonstrations which bring contention were prohibited. Opponents to the Church went to court and protested the ban on speech. Their position was that the easement allowing the general public access was considered public rather than private property and that the constitution of the United States prohibited any restrictions on what could be considered expression in a public forum. They found a sympathetic judge who ruled in their favor. Protesters arrived soon after the decision was announced with placards and bullhorns. Their shouts of obscenities disrupted the peace which was intended. The community polarized into two camps: one for releasing the easement so the Church could reinstate the tranquility; the other for abandoning or selling the easement. They desired a forum on Church property to air their grievances against the Church.

During the turmoil, Church leaders sought compromise rather than confrontation. Instead of retaliating and striking back at the mayor who refused to release the easement, reconciliation was sought. When it became apparent it was not in his best interest to keep the issue alive, when marriage parties were harassed as they tried to take pictures, the mayor championed a proposal to sell the easement to the Church. Church leaders quickly agreed to donate several valuable acres of land to the city in exchange for the city releasing the easement.

In this, when sued through the American justice system, the leaders of Christ's Church extended mercy by giving up the "cloke" after losing their "cloak." While this resolution was being negotiated, the leaders were able to concentrate on the work of the kingdom rather than the lawsuit.

Lending

> Give to him that asketh thee, and from him that would borrow of thee turn not away. (Matthew 5:42; see also 3 Nephi 12:42)

The Savior teaches another aspect of being merciful with these instructions. Leaders of Christ's kingdom are to give to those who ask and not turn away those who would borrow. Later in their ministry, the Apostles were sent out to teach the gospel without resources (see Luke 10:3–4). They would be dependent upon the Lord through others for the necessities of life. In keeping with the parable referred to earlier where the Lord showed mercy, the leaders must also show mercy to others. This is not to say that all an individual's personal wealth is to be given to the less fortunate. Church leaders are to follow the spirit of discernment, which comes with their call, to know what resources are to be distributed to which people. They should also be guided as to whether or not the resources are to be given or loaned. The concept is to be free with the abundance the Lord has given in order to further the work of exaltation.

These instructions are important for the Apostles in Palestine. The Savior continued to train his future leaders for several years. Then, after he ascended into heaven, the leaders left their vocations and directed all their energies to furthering the kingdom of God. Thus, the funds used to sustain their lives were donated to the Lord and made sacred. Yet the Savior would have his leaders assist those who were in need.

Just over a hundred years prior to the Savior's birth, a righteous king in the New World taught his people the importance of assisting those in need. In his teaching, King Benjamin put into words the mercy of God:

> And now, for the sake of these things which I have spoken unto you—that is for the sake of retaining a remission of your sins from day to day, that you may walk guiltless before God—I would that ye should impart of your substance to the poor, every man according to that which he hath, such as feeding the hungry, clothing the naked, visiting the sick and administering to their relief, both spiritually and temporally, according to their wants. (Mosiah 4:26)

This quote brings to mind the parable of the king and his unrighteous servant quoted in the introduction. If we desire God's mercy in having our sins remitted, we must be merciful to our brothers and sisters. This includes imparting, in wisdom, our substance and the Church's resources to those in need.

Since the Restoration of God's kingdom in modern times, this commandment to assist those in need has been restated (see Doctrine and Covenants 42:31; 44:6). It has become more organized in the collection of funds through fast offerings and other donations. Bishops are charged to see that those who are in need and worthy receive what is needed to sustain life. This aid is extended not just to the Saints but is sent worldwide to aid the victims of natural calamity, war, drought, or disease. By extending mercy and assisting those in need, we can obtain the mercy of God.

Law of Love

> Ye have heard that it hath been said, Thou shalt love thy neighbor, and hate thine enemy. (Matthew 5:43; see also 3 Nephi 12:43)

This is the last time the Savior would refer to the law of Moses and its accompanying traditions in the Sermon on the Mount. In this instance, instead of amplifying these laws or traditions as before, Christ is going to change them in favor of a higher law. The law of love is the ultimate act in extending mercy.

> But I say unto you, Love your enemies, bless them that curse you, do good to them that hate you, and pray for them which despitefully use you, and persecute you;
>
> That ye may be the children of your Father which is in heaven: for he maketh his sun to rise on the evil and on the good, and sendeth rain on the just and on the unjust.
>
> For if you love them which love you, what reward have ye? do not even the publicans the same?

And if ye salute your brethren only, what do ye more than others? do not even the publicans so? (Matthew 5:44–47; see also 3 Nephi 12:44–45)

The law given by Moses was to love one's neighbor while hating the enemy. Christ's instructions to his disciples were completely foreign to their experience. They were to love enemies, to bless those who curse, and to pray for persecutors. By doing this, the leaders in Christ's kingdom avoid contention and become children of Heavenly Father.

After organizing the church of Christ at the Waters of Mormon, Alma ordained priests to teach the people (see Mosiah 18:17–19). His instructions to the priests were

that there should be no contention one with another, but that they should look forward with one eye, having one faith, and one baptism, having their hearts knit together in unity and in love one towards another.

And thus he commanded them to preach. And thus they became the children of God. (Mosiah 18:21–22)

The scriptures and modern-day prophets teach that all people are literally spirit children of a loving Father in Heaven. This lineage can be broken, however. Those who choose to disregard God's teachings choose to leave God's presence and renounce their birthright. Bruce R. McConkie in his Messiah series writes,

Of olden time, and in ages past, Israel's enemies had been God's enemies, and the Gentile nations were kept away at swords point; had it not been so the chosen people would have been swallowed up by the world. Their world was one of force and violence in which whole nations were forced to believe what their rulers decreed or be destroyed from off the face of the earth. This tight grip on the minds of men has now been loosened, and now the gospel is to go to the world—all men everywhere are to hear the word. Israel must love the Gentiles, for they are to be adopted into the family of Jehovah.

All men will be judged by what is in their hearts. If their souls are full of hatred and cursings, such characteristics shall be restored to them in the resurrection. Loving one's enemies and blessing one's cursers perfects the soul. Such perfection is the object of the Gospel, and of it Jesus now chooses to speak. (*The Mortal Messiah* 2:142)

Elder James E. Talmage in *Jesus the Christ* taught,

This is new doctrine. Never before have Israel been required to love their foes. Friendship for enemies had found no place in the Mosaic code: indeed the people had grown to look upon Israel's enemies as God's enemies; and now Jesus required that tolerance, mercy, and even love be meted out to such! He supplemented the requirement by an explanation—through the course indicated by Him men may become the children of God, like unto their Heavenly Father to the extent of their obedience; for the Father is kind, long-suffering and tolerant, causing His sun to shine on the evil and on the good, and sending rain for the sustenance of both just and unjust. And further, what excellence has the man who gives only as he receives, acknowledges only those who salute him with respect, loves only as he is loved? Even the publicans did that much. Of the disciples of Christ much more was expected. (*Jesus the Christ*, p. 236)

In being merciful, the leaders of Christ's kingdom on earth are to love those who hate them just as God loves all his children, obedient and disobedient alike. The Savior reminded the brethren that they would be persecuted because they maintained the doctrines and ordinances of Christ in purity or because they had been perceived to have left the law of Moses. In spite of this persecution, leaders are expected to be merciful in all aspects. The example given is that our Father is merciful in providing sunshine and rain—items necessary in raising crops—for both the just and the unjust. He is kind and long-suffering, not harboring hate, as we must also be. Elder McConkie pointed out that all men will be judged by the contents of their hearts or what is referred to as character. The great restoration known as the Resurrection will not change or erase emotions harbored in the soul. If one hates or curses another throughout their life, those characteristics remain. It is only the body that is resurrected to a perfect, immortal state. The spirit remains as it was. To be as our Father in Heaven, leaders must be tolerant. They must be merciful in blessing enemies with the opportunity to receive the gospel. They must reach out to help those who criticize or persecute. "Loving one's enemies and blessing one's cursers' perfects the soul" as McConkie writes.

This aspect of gospel leadership was exemplified by the sons of Mosiah. Although born of nobility and heirs to the throne of the Nephites, these four men chose to love their enemy. After teaching the word of God to their own people, Ammon, Aaron, Omner, and Himni took their message to the Lamanites who were described as a wild and ferocious people who delighted in murdering the Nephites (see Alma 17:14). These four men endured hardships and persecution as they taught the gospel to their enemies. The result of this effort was that thousands of one-time enemies were brought into the fold of Christ and ended a source of conflict to their own people (see Alma 23:4–6). In this they were merciful.

There is a difference between the training given by the Savior in Palestine and that in the New World. Christ adds,

> Therefore those things which were of old time, which were under the law, in me are all fulfilled.
>
> All things are done away, and all things have become new. (3 Nephi 12:46–47)

To a related people who, separated by oceans, had different yet similar experiences and to a people who had been taught by the law of Moses to love their friends and hate enemies, the Savior taught that the law was ended. He had completed the Atonement and Resurrection, fulfilled all the necessary conditions, and all things had become new. Thus, it was time to do good to those who cursed, to love those who hated, and to pray for those who despitefully used. Thus doing, they would be merciful.

> For if ye love them which love you, what thank have ye? for sinners also love them that love them.
>
> And if ye do good to them which do good to you, what thank have ye? for sinners also do even the same.
>
> And if ye lend to them of whom ye hope to receive, what thank have ye? for sinners also lend to sinners, to receive as much again.
>
> But love ye your enemies, and do good, and lend, hoping for nothing again; and your reward shall be great, and ye shall be great, and ye shall be the children of the Highest: for he is kind unto the unthankful and to the evil.
>
> Be ye therefore merciful, as your Father also is merciful. (Luke 6:32–36)

Perfection

Up to this point in the Sermon on the Mount, the Savior has contrasted old Mosaic laws and customs with the new gospel laws. Now Christ closes this portion of training to his disciples with a comprehensive summary of what had been taught. He said,

> Ye are therefore commanded to be perfect, even as your Father which is in heaven is perfect. (Matthew 5:48 JST)

This command from the Savior to be perfect is intimidating to many because they determine it to be impossible to fulfill. Yet the scriptures specify that Noah, Seth, and Job were considered perfect men (see Genesis 6:9; Doctrine and Covenants 107:43; Job 1:1). In the Americas, Alma stated that there were an "exceeding great many who were made pure and entered God's presence" (see Alma 13:10–12). In this quick review, one can see it is possible for a person to be perfect in the sense God requires for it has been done. The Lord does not give a commandment without providing a way for those so commanded to obey (see 1 Nephi 3:7; 9:6; 17:3). By completing the atonement Christ made it possible for Just men to be made perfect (see Doctrine and Covenants 76:69).

Bruce McConkie in *Mormon Doctrine* defines what our Father in Heaven desires us to be. He writes that

> perfection is of two kinds—finite or mortal, and infinite or eternal. Finite perfection may be gained by the righteous saints in this life. It consists in living a godfearing life of devotion to the truth, of walking in complete submission to the will of the Lord, and of putting first in one's life the things of the Kingdom of God. Infinite perfection is reserved for

those who overcome all things and inherit the fulness of the Father in the mansions hereafter. It consists in gaining eternal life, the kind of life which God has in the highest heaven within the Celestial world. (*Mormon Doctrine*, p. 567)

The Savior also gave the commandment of perfection to his disciples in the Americas. But there was an addition. He taught,

Therefore I would that ye should be perfect even as I, or your Father who is in heaven is perfect. (3 Nephi 12:48)

In these instructions, Christ gives two examples of perfection for the American disciples to emulate: God the Father and his Only Begotten Son, Jesus the Christ. The Savior had completed his mortal ministry by atoning for mankind's sins, being crucified, and then being resurrected. By being obedient to God's will, Jesus completed the process and became as God is. He became perfect in the infinite sense of the definition as explained by Bruce McConkie. Although without sin and completely obedient to his Father's will (perfection in the finite definition), the Savior needed to be resurrected to be perfect in the infinite sense. But this reward is not restricted to Christ alone.

Perfection—a relative degree of perfection in this life, and eternal perfection, the kind possessed by the Father, in the life to come—these are gained by full obedience to the fulness of gospel law. This is the doctrine of exaltation, the doctrine that as God now is, man may become; this is the doctrine that mortals have power to become like Deity in power, might and dominion; in wisdom, knowledge, and truth; in love, charity, mercy, integrity, and in all holy attributes. "Ye shall be even as I am, and I am even as the Father; and the

> Father and I are one," Jesus said to certain faithful Nephites disciples (3 Nephi 28:10). (*The Mortal Messiah* 2:143)

In commanding the leaders of his kingdom to be perfect, Christ has very effectively encapsulated the teachings found in the prior Beatitudes.

> If the newly called saints overcome anger; if they are reconciled with their brethren; if they rise above lewd and lascivious thoughts and commit no adultery in their hearts; if they cast away their sins, as though severing an offending hand; if their every spoken word is true as though sworn with an oath; if they do not retaliate when others offend them; if they turn the other cheek and resist not evil impositions; if they love their enemies, bless those who curse them, and pray for those who despitefully use them and persecute them—if they do all these things, they will become perfect even as their Eternal Father is perfect. And perfection comes not by the law of Moses, but by the Gospel. (*The Mortal Messiah* 2:143)

BLESSED ARE THEY WHICH DO HUNGER AND THIRST AFTER RIGHTEOUSNESS

Blessed are they which do hunger and thirst after righteousness: for they shall be filled. (Matthew 5:6)

At this point [the Savior] is somewhat less than halfway through the Sermon on the Mount. Now he turns from contrasting the old and the new to an out-and-out proclamation of new and glorious standards" (see *The Mortal Messiah* 2:143–144). Those disciples in Palestine who were to become the leaders of Christ's Church during his absence were instructed to seek after righteousness. The imagery used to aid in understanding this concept is that of the physical appetites of hunger and thirst and is something that everyone understands regardless of culture or social standing. An individual who is hungry anticipates the next meal and seeks the opportunity to assuage that hunger. A thirsty person likewise seeks water. Thus, the disciples were told to seek after righteousness in the same manner as a person who is hungry and thirsty.

Later in his mortal ministry, Christ taught this concept to his disciples again using a different method. He taught the parable of the unjust steward. At first, we learn that this steward had not been diligent in his assignment and wasted his master's goods. Knowing that he would have the stewardship removed leaving him without means to live, the steward called the master's debtors to him and reduced the amounts owed. This was done with the hope of gaining the debtors' favor. The parable concludes with the Lord commending the steward for "he had done wisely" (see Luke 16:1–9). This commendation was not for the fraudulent manner in which the man worked to provide for his future but for his zeal. James Talmage wrote,

> Our Lord's purpose was to show the contrast between the care, thoughtfulness, and devotion of men engaged in the money-making affairs of earth, and the half hearted ways of many who are professedly striving after spiritual riches. Worldly-minded men do not neglect provision for their future years, and often are sinfully eager to amass plenty; while the "children of light," or those who believe spiritual wealth to be above all earthly possessions, are less energetic, prudent, or wise. (*Jesus the Christ*, p. 463)

Thus, Christ's disciples are to have the zeal of the unjust steward, of the scribes and Pharisees, in seeking after the kingdom of heaven which is more valuable than the wealth and praise of the world. They were to hunger and thirst after righteousness.

Earlier in the Sermon when Christ had recited the Beatitudes, he also gave a promise or a blessing. The persecuted would receive the kingdom of heaven, the peacemakers would be called the children of God, and so on. For this beatitude, Christ's disciples in Palestine received the promise of being filled if they zealously sought righteousness, but the Savior did not specify what they would be filled with. It must have been self-evident to those he taught. However, it does not appear to have been so evident in the Americas, and the Savior was more explicit in his instructions. He said,

> And blessed are all they who do hunger and thirst after righteousness, for they shall be filled with the Holy Ghost. (3 Nephi 12:6)

As it states in the first article of faith, members of The Church of Jesus Christ of Latter-day Saints believe in God the Father, in Christ, and in the Holy Ghost. Scriptures also detail that the Father and Christ have tangible bodies of flesh and bones while the Holy Ghost is a personage of spirit, which allows an individual to receive the Holy Ghost's influence (see Doctrine and Covenants 130:22–23). The promise or blessing for those who hunger and thirst after righteousness is to be filled with the Holy Ghost.

There are many reasons why being filled with the Holy Ghost is a blessing. Angels "speak by the power of the Holy Ghost" (see 2 Nephi 32:3; 33:1). One of the greatest sermons ever taught, that given by King Benjamin, came through an angel by the power of the Holy Ghost (see Mosiah 3:2). Six hundred years before the Savior's mortal ministry, the prophet Lehi had called the people of Jerusalem to repentance. As he taught, he did so with the power of the Holy Ghost. Lehi's son, Nephi, also desired to see what his father had seen and knew it would be provided through the power of the Holy Ghost. The Holy Ghost is the gift to all who diligently seek the Father and follow his commandments (see 1 Nephi 10:17). The influence of the Holy Ghost has been categorized into areas that have been termed the Gifts of the Spirit. As God is no respecter of persons any individual who obeys God's word receives the blessing. There is no discrimination for age, sex, race, or the period of time in earth's history.

As a leader in Christ's Kingdom it is very important to be worthy of the gifts of the Spirit. In *Mormon Doctrine*, Bruce R. McConkie explains about these gifts and how they can benefit an individual. He wrote,

> By the grace of God—following devotion, faith and obedience on man's part—certain spiritual blessings called *gifts of the spirit* are bestowed upon men. Their receipt is always predicated upon obedience to law, but because they are freely available to all the obedient, they are called gifts. They are signs and miracles reserved for the faithful and for none else.
>
> Moroni says that the gifts of God come from Christ, by the power of the Holy Ghost and by the Spirit of Christ (Moroni 10). In other words, the gifts come by the power of that Spirit who is the Holy Ghost, but the Spirit of Christ (or light of Christ) is the agency through which the Holy Ghost operates.
>
> Their purpose is to enlighten, encourage, and edify the faithful so that they will inherit peace in this life and be guided toward eternal life in the world to come. Their presence is proof of the divinity of the Lords work; where they are not found, there the Church and Kingdom of God is not. (*Mormon Doctrine*, p. 314)

Thus, if a leader seeks after righteousness, he or she will be rewarded with the gifts of the Spirit. These gifts are for the obedient and can be considered evidence of the Church of Christ. They are to enlighten and edify the faithful and to encourage God's children toward exaltation.

President Wilford Woodruff related an experience at the October General Conference of 1880 that stressed the importance of obtaining the Holy Spirit. In this sermon, he told of a vision he had of going to an earlier conference where he saw Brigham Young and Heber Kimball. Since both of these leaders had died years earlier, President Woodruff approached President Young and asked him to address the Saints at the conference. President Young declined but announced that he had a message for President Woodruff. He said,

> I want you to teach this people—and I want you to follow this counsel yourself—that they must labor and so live as to obtain the Holy Spirit, for without this you cannot build up the Kingdom; without the spirit of God you are in danger of walking in the dark, and in danger of failing to accomplish your calling as apostles and elders in the church and kingdom of God. And said he, Brother Joseph taught me this principle. (Wilford Woodruff, *Journals of Discourses* 21:318)

During the first worldwide leadership training meeting dated January 11, 2003, Elder Neal A. Maxwell of the Quorum of Twelve Apostles also taught the importance of the Spirit:

> Only with revelation can we do the Lord's work according to His will in His way and according to His timing.
>
> More than any other way, the Holy Ghost can reveal to us how to connect the doctrines with our personal discipleship and also how to help members of the Church to do likewise. So when we "liken" the scriptures to ourselves, the Holy Ghost is necessary to help that to happen. He can see, for instance, our sins of omission, and by the workings of conscience, we

are moved to repent of these sins as well. If we will do so, it will bring us even greater joy in this life than we have ever known. (*Worldwide Leadership Training Meeting*, p. 5)

It is through the Spirit that a leader can apply the pure doctrines of Christ in modern lives. This keeps the danger of "walking in the dark," of apostasy, far away. In order to obtain the gifts of the Spirit, which are so crucial to a leader's ability to magnify his or her calling, they must diligently seek after righteousness. Thus, they hunger and thirst after righteousness.

This process becomes an exalting cycle. An individual seeks for righteousness, obtains the ordinances, obeys the laws, and is filled with the Holy Ghost. The gifts of the Spirit fortify the individual, so a mighty change occurs in the heart (see Alma 5:14). A result of this change of heart is the desire to do good continually (see Mosiah 5:2). By doing good continually, the individual is once again filled with the Holy Ghost.

To assist his disciples in seeking after righteousness and benefiting from the Spirit, the Savior pinpointed several items of concern that touch on the "mighty change" of the heart rather than on the outward appearance. In doing this, Christ concentrated on the motivation behind an individual's actions rather than on the actions themselves. The ideals Christ associated with this beatitude are pure charity, prayer, the manner of prayer, forgiveness, and fasting. If applied with the zeal of being hungry and thirsty as taught by the Savior, each ideal becomes an aid to receiving the gifts of the Spirit.

Pure Charity

Through the ages, the Saints have been encouraged to care for those who are less fortunate in the material things of this world. During the early years of Israel the nation, King David wrote that "blessed is he that considereth the poor: the Lord will deliver him in time of trouble" (see Psalm 41:1). Hundreds of years later and thousands of miles from Palestine, the American Saints were told that if an individual desired to walk guiltless before God, he or she would impart of their substance for the assistance of the poor. This included feeding the hungry, clothing the naked, and administering to the needs of the ill (see Mosiah 4:26).

While expected to aid the poor, the Saints were cautioned to

> see that all these things are done in wisdom and order; for it is not requisite that a man should run faster than he has strength. And again, it is expedient that he should be diligent, that thereby he might win the prize; therefore, all things must be done in order. (Mosiah 4:27)

The followers of Christ are expected to be charitable toward the needy, but they are not required to impoverish themselves in the process. As the Lord teaches about assisting the less fortunate, it becomes readily apparent that he does not consider the amounts given to the poor as important as the intent behind the gift.

> And it came to pass that, as Jesus taught his disciples, he said unto them, Take heed that ye do not your alms before men, to be seen of them: otherwise ye have no reward of your Father which is in heaven. (Matthew 6:1 JST)

Another difference between the Palestinian and American Sermons becomes apparent at this point. Although the commandment to assist the poor had been known in the Americas, Christ reiterated the instructions to help those less fortunate. He said,

> Verily, verily, I say that I would that ye should do alms unto the poor; but take heed that ye do not your alms before men to be seen of them; otherwise ye have no reward of your Father who is in heaven. (3 Nephi 13:1)

As he conducted the training session for his disciples, the Savior cautioned against being charitable in order to receive the praise of the world. In providing for the poor, it is the content of the heart—the intent behind the gift—rather than the amount or value of that gift that counts. This counsel reflects the Lord's teachings to the prophet Samuel during the selection process for a king to lead Israel. The Lord cautioned the prophet not to look at a candidate's appearance but to rely on the Lord for direction. For a "man looketh on the outward appearance, but the Lord looketh on the heart" (1 Samuel 16:7).

The desire of the donor should be to help those in need rather than in creating the appearance of giving while expecting something in return. It was to be understood that if there are selfish motives for the charity, the donor could not expect any reward from the Father. The Savior continued his explanation of this ideal with a practical example:

> Therefore when thou doest thine alms, do not sound a trumpet before thee, as the hypocrites do in the synagogues and in the streets, that they may have glory of men. Verily I say unto you, They have their reward.
>
> But when thou doest alms, let not thy left hand know what thy right hand doeth:
>
> That thine alms may be in secret: and thy Father which seeth in secret himself shall reward thee openly. (Matthew 6:2–4; see also 3 Nephi 13:2–4)

Prophets of many ages have taught that being charitable to the poor is necessary and even required. However, presenting the appearance of being charitable isn't sufficient to qualify for being filled with the Spirit. Besides the giving of substance, an individual must have an actual concern for the welfare of those less fortunate. Thus, the command "when thou doest thine alms, do not sound a trumpet before thee." Our charity toward our fellowmen is not to be driven by the desire for accolades or the glory of man. Charity should be for the benefit of those in need. The Father will reward those who do their alms in secret and have the proper intent.

> In the matter of alms-giving the Master warned against, and inferentially denounced, ostentation and hypocritical display. To give to the needy is praiseworthy; but to give for the purpose of winning the praise of men is rank hypocrisy. The tossing of alms to a beggar, the pouring of offerings into the temple treasure chests, to be seen of men, and similar displays of affected liberality, were fashionable among certain classes in the time of Christ; and the same spirit is manifest today. Some there be now who cause a trumpet to be sounded, through the columns of the press perchance, or by other means of publicity, to call attention to their giving, that they may have glory of men – to win political favor, to increase their trade or influence, to get what in their estimation is worth more than that from which they part. With logical incisiveness the Master demonstrated that such givers have their reward. They have received what they bid for; what more can such men demand or consistently expect? (*Jesus the Christ*, p. 237)

These words of James Talmage regarding the teachings of the Savior in the Sermon on the Mount indicate the need for having the proper intent while assisting the poor. If a leader or an individual acts to obtain acclaim, political power, or wealth as a result of their charitable acts and calls attention to those deeds, they will have their reward from what men will give. In this sense, the donor contracts through his donation to receive political favor or increased influence and may or may not receive according to that contract. That reward will be provided by man who is well known for reneging on promises. God will be under no obligation to provide further reward.

On the other hand, our Heavenly Father promises to recognize the individual who provides for those in need out of love for their less fortunate brothers and sisters. This is the person who fulfills his or her responsibilities without fanfare or acclaim. Although these gifts are made in secret as instructed, God looks on a man's heart and rewards openly with the Spirit.

In modern times, the Lord's plan to assist the poor is more organized. Rather than the affluent being approached by the unfortunate for assistance, the Lord has called the bishop to the responsibility of caring for those people in his ward who are in need. All that is accomplished is handled with confidentiality. Even with this improvement, the intent behind those making their offerings or a leader's actions are paramount. The Savior taught the Prophet Joseph Smith and several companions about the intent of their actions. He said,

> Behold, there are many called, but few are chosen. And why are they not chosen?
>
> Because their hearts are set so much upon the things of this world, and aspire to the honors of men, that they do not learn this one lesson—

> That the rights of the priesthood are inseparably connected with the powers of heaven, and that the powers of heaven cannot be controlled nor handled only upon the principles of righteousness.
>
> That they may be conferred upon us, it is true; but when we undertake to cover our sins, or to gratify our pride, our vain ambition, or to exercise control or dominion or compulsion upon the souls of the children of men, in any degree of unrighteousness, behold, the heavens withdraw themselves; the Spirit of the Lord is grieved; and when it is withdrawn, Amen to the priesthood or the authority of man. (Doctrine and Covenants 121:24–37)

The Lord is explicit. A leader who seeks to exercise his priesthood or authority in an unworthy manner loses that priesthood or authority. That individual's heart is set more upon the desires of the world than in seeking to further the kingdom of God. Those who desire to assist the poor in their stewardships with the proper intent, although their works are done in secret, the Lord, who sees all, will provide the appropriate reward. This is in addition to the less fortunate receiving needed assistance. The charitable always retain the Spirit of the Lord.

> This concept of providing for the poor with the proper intent was reiterated to Christ's disciples later in his Palestinian ministry. It is recorded that as
>
> Jesus sat over against the treasury, and beheld how the people cast money into the treasury: and many that were rich cast in much.
>
> And there came a certain poor widow, and she threw in two mites, which make a farthing.

> And he called unto him his disciples, and saith unto them, Verily I say unto you, That this poor widow hath cast more in, than all they which have cast into the treasury:
>
> For all they did cast in of their abundance; but she of her want did cast in all that she had, even all her living. (Mark 12:41–44)

The Savior used this incident to illustrate that God the Father desired the proper intent behind charitable acts rather than an immense treasury. Those who give of their abundance in order to receive a greater benefit from men have received their reward. The widow who cast in the least amount was counted the greatest because she cast in all that she had and exhibited pure charity.

Years later in Palestine, the Apostle Paul in his first letter to the Corinthians wrote of the importance of charity:

> Though I speak with the tongues of men and of angels, and have not charity, I am become as brass, or a tinkling cymbal.
>
> And though I have the gift of prophecy, and understand all mysteries, and all knowledge; and though I have all faith, so that I could remove mountains, and have not charity, I am nothing.
>
> And though I bestow all my goods to feed the poor, and though I give my body to be burned, and have not charity, it profiteth me nothing.
>
> Charity suffereth long, and is kind; charity envieth not; charity vaunted not itself, is not puffed up,
>
> Doth not behave itself unseemly, seeketh not her own, is not easily provoked, thinketh no evil;
>
> Rejoiceth not in iniquity, but rejoiceth in the truth;

> Beareth all things, believeth all things, hopeth all things, endureth all things. (1 Corinthians 13:1–7)

Moroni, an American prophet who saw his people destroyed, taught that

> charity suffereth long, and is kind, and envieth not, and is not puffed up, seeketh not her own, is not easily provoked, thinketh no evil, and rejoiceth not in iniquity but rejoiceth in the truth, beareth all things, believeth all things, hopeth all things, endureth all things.
>
> Wherefore, my beloved brethren, if ye have not charity, ye are nothing, for charity never faileth. Wherefore, cleave unto charity, which is the greatest of all, for all things must fall.
>
> But charity is the pure love of Christ, and it endureth forever; and whoso is found possessed of it at the last day, it shall be well with him. (Moroni 7:45–47)

Those who offer their substance for the assistance of the poor with the proper intent exhibit charity, the pure love of Christ, and are blessed with the Holy Ghost. But there is more: "at the last day, it shall be well with him."

Prayer of Faith

The idea of having the proper intent behind actions is not restricted to charity but continues into the next ideal that Christ taught to his disciples: prayer. Bruce R. McConkie taught that prayer is

> to speak with God, either vocally or by forming the thoughts involved in the mind. Prayers may properly include expressions of praise, thanksgiving, and adoration; they are solemn

occasions during which the children of God petition their Eternal Father for those things, both temporal and spiritual, which they feel are needed to sustain them in all the varied tests of this mortal probation. Prayers are occasions of confession—occasions when in humility and contrition, having broken hearts and contrite spirits, the saints confess their sins to Deity and implore him to grant his cleansing forgiveness. (*Mormon Doctrine*, p. 581)

Prayer was not a new invention at the time of Christ or at the time of Moses, Abraham, or Noah. It was introduced to our first parents in the Garden of Eden. After being exiled from the garden, an angel called upon Adam to repent and call upon God for all that was needed (see Moses 5:8). Adam followed that direction and set up his household based on revelations received from God. His children were also taught to pray.

Since that time, individuals, patriarchs, and prophets have sought guidance from God and all have received answers through revelation. Noah began construction of an ark that saved humanity from the flood, the family of Jared was spared the confounding of their language, and Lehi and his family were saved from the destruction of Jerusalem. Isaiah, Ezekiel, and Jeremiah likewise received directives from God as a result of prayer.

In modern times the restoration of gospel truths, priesthood, and saving ordinances came about because of the simple, sincere prayer of a young Joseph Smith. This is an example where prayer "is essential if men are to be saved; there is no salvation without prayer. How could a man set his heart on righteousness, so as to work out his salvation, without communing by prayer with Him who is the author of righteousness?" (*Mormon Doctrine*, p. 581).

Prayer is not to be restricted to the prophets and apostles. The Saints were also encouraged to pray. In the Americas, the prophet Nephi taught his people that if they listened "unto the Spirit which teacheth a man to pray" they would know that they must pray. In opposition to the Spirit, the adversary is also aware of the importance of prayer: "For the evil spirit teacheth not a man to pray, but teacheth him that he must not pray" (2 Nephi 32:8).

Besides teaching or influencing an individual to pray, the Spirit is also a reward. During the Restoration of the gospel, the Prophet Joseph Smith was taught that "the Spirit shall be given unto you by the prayer of faith" (Doctrine and Covenants 42:14). A prayer, a sincere prayer of faith, is rewarded by the Father with the Spirit. And with the Spirit comes inspiration and revelation. These items are essential for the exaltation of an individual and for a leader to fulfill his or her stewardship.

In the Sermon on the Mount, the Savior taught his disciples the importance of the prayer of faith. Just as with the ideal of pure charity, those who use prayer to further their career or social standing will not receive the reward of the Spirit or a desired reward in the life to come. The reward for these hypocrites is what they contracted: the temporary acclaim of man.

Leaders are often concerned about the welfare of individuals. These matters are confidential and are not to be publicly disclosed. Thus, a leader is to enter their closet and pray in secret. The Father who "seeth in secret shall reward thee openly." Christ taught that

> when thou prayest, thou shalt not be as the hypocrites are: for they love to pray standing in the synagogues and in the corners of the streets, that they may be seen of men. Verily I say unto you, They have their reward.

> But thou, when thou prayest, enter into thy closet, and when thou hast shut the door, pray to the Father which is in secret; and thy Father which seeth in secret shall reward thee openly.
>
> But when ye pray, use not vain repetitions, as the heathen do: for they think that they shall be heard for their much speaking.
>
> Be not ye therefore like unto them: for your Father knoweth what things ye have need of, before ye ask him. (Matthew 6:5–8; see also 3 Nephi 13:5–8)

In addition to mentioning the necessity of praying in seclusion, the Savior identified two areas to be wary of: vain repetitions and much speaking. Elder Spencer W. Kimball asked,

> How often do we hear people who wax eloquent in their prayers to the extent of preaching a complete sermon? The hearers tire and the effect is lost, and I sometimes wonder if perhaps the dial of the heavenly radio is not turned off when long and wordy prayers are sent heavenward. I feel sure that there is too much to do in heaven for the Lord and his servants to sit indefinitely listening to verbose praises and requests, for as we are told in Matthew, he knows, before we ask, our needs and desires. (*The Teachings of Spencer W. Kimball*, p. 119–120)

Bruce R. McConkie discussed vain repetition in terms of written prayers or phrases that are commonly read or repeated. He said that those items

> are devoid of the true spirit of prayer and should be shunned. Frequently they are spoken without real intent; and their use

keeps men from searching their own hearts in an attempt to pray in faith according to an approved pattern so that actual blessings may be granted from Deity. Not infrequently these prepared prayers are read, recited or chanted in ritualistic ceremonies in which the speakers do not concentrate all the faculties of their whole souls upon the prayers being offered. As a consequence the words often take on the nature of useless jargon and do not open the door to the receipt of the Lord's Blessings. (*Mormon Doctrine*, p. 585–586)

At the beginning of this ideal, Christ recalled to mind the hypocrites who prayed, standing in the street, to be seen of men. In these instructions, he instructed the leaders of his kingdom to retire to their closets, far from the eyes of man, to seek their God. As with pure charity, it is the intent of the prayer that matters. Thus, whether in the street or a closet, kneeling, standing, or sitting, the physical position is less important than the spiritual submission to God (refer to Russell M. Nelson, *Ensign*, May 2003, p. 7). It is the sincere prayer seeking with a humble heart that reaches the heavens and elicits answers.

An example of vain repetitions is found among the Zoramites. On the day designated for worship, each Zoramite would ascend a stand called the Rameumpton until at the top, high above the rest of the congregation. This stand was placed in the center of the Zoramites' synagogues so all present could see and hear. Once atop the stand, each person would recite the same prayer word for word. At the conclusion of their meeting, the people would return to their homes, never speaking of their god. The next time they met, the Zoramites would repeat the process (see Alma 31:12–32). Alma the high priest learned about the wickedness and pride of the people and sought to have them return to Christ. The Zoramites rejected Alma's calls for repentance and eventually joined the Lamanites, losing what connections they had with God's kingdom. Thus, prayers with vain repetitions or prayers that use many words to impress man have no power. They do not ascend to heaven because the supplicant does not wish an answer from God. Their desire is only for the recognition and praise of man. President Joseph F. Smith touched on this subject when he said,

> My brethren and sisters, do not learn to pray with your lips only. Do not learn a prayer, and say it every morning and evening. That is something I dislike very much. It is true that a great many people fall into the rut of saying over a ceremonious prayer. They begin at a certain point, and they touch at all the points along the road until they get to the winding up scene; and when they have done, I do not know whether the prayer has ascended beyond the ceiling of the room or not. (*Gospel Doctrine*, p. 220)

The Savior, in this portion of the Sermon on the Mount, is stressing the need for sincerity and real intent in their prayers to his disciples. It is these heartfelt prayers that ascend to heaven and are answered. There is power, peace, and comfort in prayers that are offered as Christ taught. An example of this power in prayer is also found in the Book of Mormon. After teaching the people in the land of Bountiful, the Savior encouraged the leaders of his church to pray:

> And it came to pass that when Jesus had thus prayed unto the Father, he came unto his disciples, and behold, they did still continue, without ceasing, to pray unto him; and they did not multiply many words, for it was given unto them what they should pray, and they were filled with desire.

> And it came to pass that Jesus blessed them as they did pray unto him; and his countenance did smile upon them, and the light of his countenance did shine upon them, and behold they were as white as the countenance and also the garments of Jesus; and behold the whiteness thereof did exceed all the whiteness, yea, even there could be nothing upon earth so white as the whiteness thereof. (3 Nephi 19:24–25)

In his instructions, the Savior warned to "not be as the hypocrites are." Bishops, Relief Society presidents (*these are positions of responsibility in the Church*), and other leaders are not to seek the acclaim of men through public and verbose prayer but to express their desires in secret prayer. By so doing, the power of prayer is unleashed. In this scripture, as his disciples prayed with real intent, the Spirit of God was present, and "it was given unto them what they should pray." In addition to receiving the Spirit, the disciples had their sins forgiven, and they were transfigured, becoming as white as the Savior.

The Savior also taught that the "Father which seeth in secret shall reward . . . openly." One of the elements Christ emphasized was praying in secret to allow the inner desires and concerns of the leader to be spoken without fear of ridicule or hope for praise. Another aspect in the use of secret prayer is that the public would not be aware of the issues facing the leader. While it is appropriate for prayers to include individuals and their difficulties, it is not appropriate for that concern to be made public. Care must be taken to maintain confidentiality when confessions are made.

A final element in proper prayer is to avoid vain repetitions, trite phrases, or the multiplying of words. The Father is not impressed with flowery phrases or many words. He seeks instead intent and the subordination of man's will to his. One of the rewards for obeying this counsel is receiving the presence of the Holy Ghost.

Manner of Prayer

After encouraging his disciples to strive for power in prayer, the Savior gave an example of those teachings in what has become known as the Lord's Prayer. In this example, he is not presenting a prayer to be recited for that would fall under the category of vain repetitions. Rather, Christ is teaching the manner of or providing a format for prayer. President Joseph F. Smith said,

> It is not good for us to pray by rote, to kneel down and repeat the Lord's prayer continually. I think that one of the greatest follies I have ever witnessed is the foolish custom of men repeating the Lord's prayer continually without considering its meaning. The Lord gave this as a pattern to his disciples who were going out into the world to preach the gospel. It was to show them that they were not to use many words but were to come directly to the Lord, and ask him for the things they might need. (*Gospel Doctrine*, p. 221)

The Savior begins the sample prayer by addressing and reverencing God the Father. He reminds his disciples that God is indeed the father of all nations, kindreds, tongues and peoples. Christ said,

> After this manner therefore pray ye: Our Father which art in heaven, Hallowed be thy name. (Matthew 6:9; see also 3 Nephi 13:9)

In referencing this portion of the Lord's Prayer, James Talmage wrote that

> in this we acknowledge the relation we bear to our Heavenly Father, and while reverencing His great and holy name, we avail ourselves of the inestimable privilege of approaching Him, less

> with the thought of His infinite glory as the Creator of all that is, the Supreme Being above all Creation, than with the loving realization that He is Father, and that we are His children. This is the earliest Biblical scripture giving instruction, permission, or warrant, for addressing God directly as 'Our Father'. Therein is expressed the reconciliation of the human family, estranged through sin, may attain by the means provided through the well beloved Son. This instruction is equally definite in demonstrating the brotherhood between Christ and humanity. As He prayed so pray we to the same Father, we as brethren and Christ as our Elder Brother. (*Jesus the Christ*, p. 238–239)

Prayers begin by calling upon the Father. With the preamble given Christ continued with the sample prayer.

> Thy Kingdom come. Thy will be done in earth, as it is in heaven. (Matthew 6:10)

When this portion of the sample prayer was given in the land Bountiful, the Savior made some changes. First, the phrase "thy kingdom come" was left out. Second, Christ asked that God's will be done "on" earth rather than "in" earth. While the second alteration is minor and deals with semantics, the first is more substantive and telling. As in other changes, the difference between the two renditions of this training has to do with the time when each sermon was presented. In Palestine, this Sermon was taught at the beginning of Christ's mortal ministry, while that given in the Americas was after the Atonement and Resurrection had been accomplished. Elder Talmage wrote,

> The Kingdom of God is to be a Kingdom of order, in which toleration and the recognition of individual rights shall prevail.

One who really prays that this Kingdom come will strive to hasten its coming by living according to the law of God. His effort will be to keep himself in harmony with the order of the kingdom, to subject the flesh to the spirit, selfishness to altruism, and to learn to love the things that God loves. To make the will of God supreme on earth as it is in heaven is to be allied with God in the affairs of life. There are many who profess belief that as God is omnipotent, all that is is according to his will. Such a supposition is unscriptural, unreasonable, and untrue. Wickedness is not in harmony with His will; falsehood, hypocrisy, vice and crime are not God's gifts to man. By His will these monstrosities that have developed as hideous deformities in human nature and life shall be abolished, and this blessed consummation shall be reached when by choice, without surrender or abrogation of their free agency, men shall do the will of God. (*Jesus the Christ*, p. 239)

The kingdom of God is one of order. It comes about as God's children use their agency to choose to obey God's will. At the time this format for prayer was presented by the Savior to his disciples in Palestine, the Atonement had not yet been accomplished. As a result, mankind was still estranged from their Heavenly Father. Thus, Christ prayed for God's kingdom to come and that he, God's only begotten in the flesh, would do his Father's will. The only way God's kingdom could come was for the Atonement to be completed.

By the time the disciples in the New World received these instructions, the Atonement had been completed. The Savior's resurrection was physically confirmed as those in the land Bountiful actually touched the Savior's scars which resulted from the Crucifixion (see 3 Nephi

11:12–15). In this sense, God's kingdom had already been established for God's children could now return to live with their Father. Christ was the epitome of the last sentence in this portion of the prayer. His actions agreed with his desire that God's will be done on earth as it is in heaven.

After Christ's ascension into heaven, it was promised that he would return (see Acts 1:9–11). This brings an added meaning to the expressed desire for Christ's kingdom to come. The Lord's disciples were to look forward to his return and, with that return, the establishment of an earthly kingdom (see Daniel 7:13–14). As Talmage points out in the above quote, those who seek for the Savior's kingdom to come will hasten its coming by adhering to the laws of God. They will follow Christ's example and subordinate their will to that of the Father.

The next phrase covered as Christ taught the manner of prayer is where he asks God the Father to "give us this day our daily bread" (Matthew 6:11).

James Talmage explains that

> food is indispensable to life. As we need it we should ask for it. True, the Father knows our need before we ask, but by asking we acknowledge Him as the Giver, and are made humble, grateful, contrite, and reliant by the request. Though the sun shines and the rain falls alike upon the just and the unjust, the righteous man is grateful for these blessings, the ungodly man receives the benefits as a matter of course with a soul incapable of gratitude. The capacity to be grateful is a blessing, for the possession of which we should be further grateful. We are taught to pray day by day for the food we need, not for a great store to be laid by for the distant future. Israel in the desert received manna as a daily supply, and

> were kept in mind of their reliance upon Him who gave. The man with much finds it easier to forget his dependence than he who must ask with each succeeding day of need. (*Jesus the Christ*, p. 239-240)

Through this phrase in the Lord's Prayer, the disciples in Palestine were taught that they would need to look to God the Father for their sustenance. This need would become more apparent as the Savior's ministry continued. Soon after receiving these instructions, the twelve Apostles were ordained and sent forth to teach of Christ and his gospel. Their assignment was to concentrate on disseminating the gospel rather than earning money for their own sustenance (see Matthew 10:5-11; Mark 6:8-10; Luke 9:1-4). As they accepted this charge, the Apostles were assured that God would be mindful of his faithful servants and would provide all that is needed. This promise is not limited to the leaders in Palestine but extends to all leaders of all times. The aid may take the form of miracles such as manna from heaven or donations from those being taught and members of the Church. But the Lord will provide what is needed.

At first, the Apostles were sent to teach the house of Israel. But when the Atonement had been completed and the Savior ascended to be with his Father, the charge was expended. The gospel was to be taken to all nations (see Matthew 28:16-20). As with their first missionary assignment to the house of Israel, the Apostles were to be concerned with taking care of the kingdom of God rather than making a living.

For the disciples in the Americas, the Lord once again adjusted his instructions. Many years earlier, American prophets taught the Saints of their lands to pray over their flocks, fields, and everything else. The disciples at the time of Christ were not told to pray for their daily needs. Nor were they instructed to preach the gospel to any but their own peoples. The American disciples were to have charge over the American Church, but their stewardship was not so large as to prevent them from providing for themselves.

Another consideration for this change in the Savior's teachings may have been a concern about priestcraft. This term refers to a practice when individuals use their own brand of religion to have the public finance a luxurious way of life. After having been warned about and experiencing the evils of priestcraft (see Alma 1), the American Saints may have been wary of any indication of that particular evil returning.

With the restoration of the gospel in modern times, the command to take Christ's word and ordinances to the entire world was reiterated. In a revelation given to Joseph Smith and Oliver Cowdery, the Lord called the two men into full-time service in order to translate the scriptures and teach the gospel. The Savior's intention was for the two men to concentrate on furthering God's work rather than on their own maintenance. Christ said,

> And thou shalt take no purse nor scrip, neither staves, neither two coats, for the Church shall give unto thee in the very hour what thou needest for food and for raiment, and for shoes and for money, and for scrip.
>
> For thou art called to prune my vineyard with a mighty pruning, yea, even for the last time; yea, and also all those whom thou has ordained, and they shall do even according to this pattern. Amen. (Doctrine and Covenants 24:18–19)

As shown in the pattern of the Palestinian and restored Churches, only those leaders so designated and called to serve the Lord full time will not be required to work for their own sustenance. In that instance, if something is needed, the Lord will provide, not in excess but what is needed. Hence the plea in the Lord's Prayer for daily bread.

> And forgive us our debts, as we forgive our debtors. (Matthew 6:12; see also 3 Nephi 13:11)

This next phrase of the sample prayer refers to the teachings regarding those of being merciful. In that beatitude, Christ taught that God would be merciful with those who were merciful in turn. This is such an important principle that the Savior also discusses it in the current beatitude. His sample prayer reminds the supplicant that God will forgive as others are forgiven. This concept is also reviewed one more time when the Savior has finished with the prayer.

Elder Talmage explained this phrase when he wrote that

> he who can thus pray with full intent and unmixed purpose merits forgiveness. In this specification of personal supplication we are taught to expect only as we deserve. The selfish and sinful would rejoice in exemption from their lawful debts, but being selfish and sinful would exact the last farthing from those who owe them. Forgiveness is too precious a pearl to be cast at the feet of the unforgiving; and, without the sincerity that springs from a contrite heart, no man may justly claim mercy. If others owe us, either in actual money or goods as suggested by debts and debtors, or through some infringement upon our rights included under the broader designation as a trespass, our mode of dealing with them will be taken into righteous accounts in the judgment of our own offences. (*Jesus the Christ*, p. 240)

The final portion of this final prayer is

> and suffer us not to be led into temptation, but deliver us from evil: For thine is the kingdom, and the power, and the glory, forever. Amen. (Matthew 6:13 JST)

When Christ recounted this portion of the prayer to his American disciples, he made another alteration. The phrase "and suffer us not to be led into temptation" was changed to "and lead us not into temptation" (see 3 Nephi 13:12). One interpretation of the American version intimates that God might lead an individual into temptation or evil in a capricious manner while the Palestinian version is a request that the Father prevent his children from experiencing temptation completely. Thus, the supplicant is to be delivered from evil. Both of these interpretations are wrong. The plan for the exaltation of mankind allows for the presence of temptation to test and prove God's children. This test would provide the opportunity for one individual to gain the necessary spiritual strength to become as God is by properly exercising one's agency and overcoming temptation (see Abraham 3:5). James Talmage wrote that

> we are not to understand that God would ever lead a man into temptation except, perhaps, by way of wise permission, to test and prove him, thereby affording him opportunity of overcoming and so of gaining spiritual strength, which is the only true advancement in man's eternal course of progress....
>
> The intent of the supplication appears to be that we be preserved from temptation beyond our weak powers to withstand; that we be not abandoned to temptation without the divine support that shall be as full a measure of

> protection as our exercise of choice will allow. (*Jesus the Christ*, p. 240–241)

God does not "lead" anyone into temptation but allows an individual to be tempted as a means by which the person is proven worthy of greater blessings. This is all based upon the individual's exercise of agency. A consolation for mankind is that God will not allow a temptation greater than a person is able to withstand. In a general epistle to the twelve tribes of Israel, James wrote,

> Blessed is the man that resisteth temptation for when he is tried, he shall receive the crown of life, which the Lord hath promised to them that love him.
>
> Let no man say when he is tempted, I am tempted of God: for God cannot be tempted with evil, neither tempted he any man:
>
> But every man is tempted, when he is drawn away of his own lust, and enticed. (James 1:12–14)

Paul in his first letter to the Corinthians wrote,

> There hath no temptation taken you but such as is common to man: but God is faithful, who will not suffer you to be tempted above that ye are able; but will with the temptation also make a way to escape, that ye may be able to bear it. (1 Corinthians 10:13)

In the Americas, as he taught the people of Ammonihah, the prophet Alma said,

> But that ye would humble yourselves before the Lord, and call on his holy name, and watch and pray continually, that ye

may not be tempted above that which ye can bear, and thus be led by the Holy Spirit, becoming humble, meek, submissive, patient, full of love and all long-suffering. (Alma 13:28)

The conclusion that can be drawn from these verses is that God will not lead an individual into temptation. God forcing someone into a certain path abrogates that individual's agency which existed prior to this mortal existence (see Helaman 14:30–31; Moses 7:32). God will allow a person to experience temptation as a means for growth. But he will not allow man to be tempted beyond the ability to resist. For that, too, would abrogate man's agency.

With that said, a person should not seek out temptation. Those who do so have no promise of deliverance. James Talmage wrote,

> How inconsistent then to go, as many do, into the places where the temptations to which we are most susceptible are strongest; for the man beset with a passion for strong drink to so pray and then resort to the dramshop; for the man whose desires are lustful to voice such a prayer and then go where lust is kindled; for the dishonest man, though he say the prayer, to then place himself where he knows the opportunity to steal will be found! Can such souls as these be other than hypocrites in asking God to deliver them from the evils they have sought? Temptation will fall in our way without our seeking, and evil will present itself even when we desire most to do right; for deliverance from such we may pray with righteous expectation and assurance. (*Jesus the Christ*, p. 241)

The final phrase of Christ's sample prayer once again acknowledges the being to whom this world and all therein belongs. It was at the command of God the Father that the universe came to be (see Moses 1:33; Acts 17:24). Then, after all things required have been accomplished, all the kingdoms of men will become the kingdom of God to be ruled forever by Christ (see Revelations 11:15).

This closing also acknowledges from whence all priesthood power comes and assigns all glory to the Father. Once again, the objective is to submit man's will to that of God. During his mortal ministry, Christ said that all his actions and miracles were performed for the glory of the Father (see John 7:18; 8:50). Christ's attitude of being submissive to the Father was present even prior to his birth into mortality (see Moses 4:2). Those who do likewise receive the promised blessing and shall be filled with the Holy Ghost.

Forgiveness

With the instructions regarding prayer concluded and a sample prayer provided, the Savior comes back to an item mentioned in that prayer. He discusses the topic of forgiveness. In the beatitude regarding mercy, Christ taught that if one desired to receive God's mercy, mercy must be shown to others. This principle pertains to forgiveness. In the sample prayer, the Lord taught his disciples to pray for forgiveness of their debts as they forgave the debts of others. Now, the Savior reiterates that idea.

> For if ye forgive men their trespasses, your heavenly Father will also forgive you:
> But if ye forgive not men their trespasses, neither will your Father forgive your trespasses. (Matthew 6:14–15; see also 3 Nephi 13:14–15)

Later, in his mortal ministry, the Savior rode into Jerusalem amid shouts of praise from its inhabitants. During this visit, he drove the moneychangers from the temple and cursed a fig tree. Amidst these events, he took the time to teach again the principle of forgiveness to Peter. Christ said,

> And when ye stand praying, forgive, if ye have ought against any: that your Father also which is in heaven may forgive you your trespasses.
> But if ye do not forgive, neither will your Father which is in heaven forgive your trespasses. (Mark 11:25–26)

Many years before Christ ministered in Palestine, the prophet Alma taught his people to forgive those who sought forgiveness. He said,

> And ye shall also forgive one another your trespasses; for verily I say unto you, he that forgiveth not his neighbors trespasses when he says that he repents, the same hath brought himself under condemnation. (Mosiah 26:31)

Besides teaching this concept to his leaders in Palestine and in the land Bountiful, Christ taught his modern disciples. In a revelation given to Joseph Smith for the benefit of the elders in Kirtland, Ohio, the Lord said,

> Wherefore, I say unto you, that ye ought to forgive one another; for he that forgiveth not his brother his trespasses standeth condemned before the Lord; for there remaineth in him the greater sin.
> I, the Lord, will forgive whom I will forgive, but of you it is required to forgive all men. (Doctrine and Covenants 64:9–10)

The principle taught in the lesson regarding mercy and reiterated here is that if an individual desires the blessings of mercy and forgiveness, it will not be granted if the individual cannot grant mercy and forgiveness to others. In addition, it is required that all must forgive those who truly desire that blessing. This forgiveness must be sincere not feigned. Elder Spencer W. Kimball, in his book *The Miracle of Forgiveness*, wrote,

> Many people, when brought to a reconciliation with others, say they forgive, but they continue to hold malice, continue to suspect the other party, continue to disbelieve the others sincerity. This is sin, for when a reconciliation has been effected and when repentance is claimed, each should forgive and forget, build immediately the fences which have been breached, and restore the former capability.
>
> The early disciples evidently expressed words of forgiveness, and on the surface made the required adjustment, but 'forgave not on another in their hearts'. This was not a forgiveness, but savored of hypocrisy and deceit and subterfuge. As implied in Christ's model prayer, it must be a heart action and a purging of one's mind. Forgiveness means forgetfulness. One woman had 'gone through' a reconciliation in a branch and made the physical motions and verbal statements indicating it, and expressed the mouthy words forgiving. Then with flashing eyes, she remarked, 'I will forgive her, but I have a memory like an elephant. I'll never forget.' Her pretended adjustment was valueless and void. She still harbored the bitterness. Her words of friendship were as straw, and she herself continued to suffer without peace of mind. Worse still, she stood 'condemned before the Lord', and there remained in her an even greater sin than in the one who, she claimed, had injured her.

> Little did this antagonistic woman realize that she had not forgiven at all. She had only made motions. She was spinning her wheels and getting nowhere. In the scripture quoted above, the phrase 'in their hearts' has deep meaning. It must be a purging of feelings and thoughts and bitternesses. Mere words avail nothing. (*The Miracle of Forgiveness*, p. 262–263)

For a leader of Christ's kingdom to be forgiven of their own shortcomings and missteps, they must extend forgiveness to others. In the previous quote, Elder Kimball referred to a woman who made the motions of but did not extend true forgiveness. He did not advocate leaving out the words or ignoring the motions of forgiveness. The outward manifestations must be present. But for the motions and the words to have any meaning at all, an inner change must occur. There must be a "purging of feelings and thoughts and bitternesses." This is the forgetting Elder Kimball references.

When a leader extends forgiveness and "forgets" the wrong or injury, care must be exercised. They should not subject themselves or the Church to the same wrong or injury from others or a repeat injury from the initial offending individual. In the April 2003 General Conference, Elder David E. Sorenson of the Presidency of the Seventy said,

> I would like to make it clear that forgiveness of sins should not be confused with tolerating evil. In fact, in the Joseph Smith Translation, the Lord said, 'Judge righteous judgment'. The Savior asks us to forsake and combat sin in all its forms, and although we must forgive a neighbor who injures us, we should still work constructively to prevent that injury from being repeated. A woman who is abused should not seek revenge, but neither should she feel that she cannot

take steps to prevent further abuse. A businessman treated unfairly in a transaction should not hate the person who was dishonest but could take appropriate steps to remedy the wrong. Forgiveness does not require us to accept and tolerate evil. It does not require us to ignore the wrong that we see in the world around us or in our own lives. But as we fight against sin, we must not allow hatred or anger to control our thoughts or actions. (*Conference Report*, April 2003)

An example of proper forgiveness is shown in the story of Joseph sold into Egypt. Because of jealousy, his older brothers threatened to take his life then settled for selling him into slavery. As a result, Joseph was taken into Egypt and became property of an official for Pharaoh. Through diligence in duty and blessings from God he rose into prominence in the household of Potiphar before being cast into prison on false charges. Rather than be consumed with hatred and bitterness for being unjustly imprisoned, he trusted in the Lord and began anew.

Because of Joseph's obedience to God's laws and following the Spirit, he was released from prison and attained a rank second only to that of Pharaoh. Once in a position this powerful, some people would have taken the opportunity to exact vengeance on those who had injured them. But that would not have shown the forgiveness that God requires. Joseph did not seek retribution against those who had cast him wrongly into prison but forgave them and improved the lives of the entire realm of Egypt.

Some years later, during a time of famine, the brothers who had sold Joseph into slavery came to Egypt seeking food. Because the storing and distribution of food was under his care, the sons of Jacob were brought before Joseph. The years and the hardship had changed his countenance enough that even his family failed to recognize him. This was another opportunity for him to exact vengeance. But, once again, Joseph reaffirmed his forgiveness and brought his family to live with him in Egypt (see Genesis 37, 39–45). Joseph's actions changed bitterness to love. He "forgot."

A leader in Christ's kingdom should likewise seek to purge bitterness, hatred, and anger from their lives as Joseph did. This is true forgiveness. When they forgive others their trespasses, they become eligible to have their own weaknesses forgiven. Then they are filled with the Holy Ghost.

Fasting

Bruce R. McConkie, in his book *Mormon Doctrine*, wrote that

> fasting, with prayer as its companion, is designed to increase spirituality; to foster a spirit of devotion and love of God; to increase faith in the hearts of men, thus assuring divine favor; to encourage humility and contrition of soul; to aid in the acquirement of righteousness; to teach man his nothingness and dependence upon God; and to hasten those who properly comply with the law of fasting along the path to salvation. (*Mormon Doctrine*, p. 276)

The elements of a proper fast are to have a reason for the fast, pray to communicate that reason to our Father in Heaven, and refrain from food and drink for a period of time. Funds saved from not eating are to be contributed to the assistance of the poor. The time for a fast has been suggested to be one day or two meals. Individuals with medical problems or are nursing children should use wisdom in fasting. Those who follow the guidelines for fasting receive pleasure in their fast (see Isaiah 58:3). This principle is to be used to "loose the bands of wickedness, to undo the heavy burdens, and to let the oppressed go free, and that ye break every yoke" (Isaiah 58:6).

It is intended that those who hunger and thirst after righteousness will use fasting in joint action with prayer to increase their spirituality. For "fasting, coupled with mighty prayer, is powerful. It can fill our minds with the revelations of the Spirit. It can strengthen us against times of temptation" (see Joseph B. Wirthlin, *Ensign*, May 2001, p. 73). Through the use of this principle, a person can attune his or her desires and attitudes toward the Father and prepare themselves to receive instructions from on high. Thus, it is appropriate that Christ completed this beatitude regarding a sincere desire for righteousness by instructing his disciples about fasting. He said,

> Moreover when ye fast, be not, as the hypocrites, of a sad countenance: for they disfigure their faces, that they may appear unto men to fast. Verily I say unto you, They have their reward.
>
> But thou, when thou fastest, anoint thine head, and wash thy face;
>
> That thou appear not unto men to fast, but unto thy Father which is in secret: and thy Father, which seeth in secret, shall reward thee openly. (Matthew 6:16–18; see also 3 Nephi 13:16–18)

Once again, the Savior instructs the leaders of his kingdom to be more interested in the intent of a righteous deed rather than its form. The disciples were to appear as normal as possible when they fasted. This practice was the opposite of the hypocrites of the time who drew attention to their "pious" fast. As with charity and prayer, those who fast and make a spectacle of it to receive the acclaim of men receive no lasting benefit.

The hypocrite's desire is not for spirituality or an increase in faith. They may not even desire a resolution of the problem for which the fasting was initiated. Their desire is for an increase in fame, wealth, or power. Thus, there is no power in their "fast." Rather, it is just going hungry.

In this ideal, the Savior desired his disciples to seek for power in their fast rather than the acclaim of the public. Regarding this matter, James Talmage wrote "that to be of avail Fasting must be a matter between the man and his God, not between man and his kind" (*Jesus the Christ*, p. 242). For a Church leader to be successful in his or her stewardship, they must seek the Lord through fasting and prayer. This will assist the leader by increasing his or her spirituality and faith as well as being filled with the Holy Ghost. The acquiring of righteousness and the gifts of the Spirit will allow the leader to further Christ's kingdom as he would have it done.

Summary

This beatitude begins the portion of the Sermon on the Mount that does not reference the law of Moses. Rather, it introduces a higher law. "Blessed are those who seek after righteousness" refers to those who desire to have the spiritual man overcome the natural and to submit their own desires to God. As they do so, they become closer to receiving their own exaltation. In addition, a part of a leader's stewardship is to encourage and assist those in their care toward their own exaltation. A needed aid in this effort is the Holy Ghost. The promise is that those who sincerely strive to obey God's laws, to hunger and thirst after righteousness, will be filled with the Holy Ghost.

In order to encourage being receptive to the Holy Ghost, the Savior outlined several ideals for his disciples. Although there are many items which encourage sensitivity to direction from the Spirit, Christ taught about pure charity, prayer and the manner of prayer, forgiveness, and fasting.

The last ideal for this beatitude is fasting. Elder Wirthlin pointed out that fasting is a powerful tool for a leader in Christ's kingdom. It can assist in receiving revelation or in resisting temptation. These and other blessings can only be received if the intent for fasting is pure. Those who make a show of pious fasting to receive the acclaim of men do not have power in their fast. They are just hungry.

After providing an example of sincere prayer and its contents, the Savior returned to an item mentioned in the prayer: forgiveness. In his teachings, the disciples are taught once again that to be forgiven of their own sins, the disciples must extend forgiveness to others. This operates on the same principle as receiving mercy. Those who refuse to forgive the truly repentant are guilty of a sin greater than the original offense. They commit the sin of unforgiving. Once again, the Savior seeks for substance rather than form. The charge is to truly forgive rather than just go through the motions.

The second ideal Christ taught involves prayer as the preeminent method of communication provided to enhance and strengthen a relationship with the Father. It assists in providing answers when questions are asked, comfort and solace in times of distress, and an opportunity to express gratitude for blessings already received. Prayer is to be pure communication with the Father and will be aided and rewarded with the Holy Ghost.

Although prayer is used for communicating with our Heavenly Father, there are impediments to receiving the desired blessing. If an individual prays in public, seeking the attention of the masses similar to the techniques used by the hypocrites, like using many words or repetitions, the Spirit is lost. This type of prayer is not seeking the favor of God but desires acceptance of men. Christ wanted his disciples to be blessed by God rather than praised by man. The Holy Ghost and the assistance he provides is much more valuable, particularly when considered in the aspect of Church service. Therefore, the intent of the prayer should be for the leader to seek the mind and will of God as well as seek the benefit of His children. If this occurs the Spirit will be present.

As an aid in having meaningful prayer and a successful communication with our Heavenly Father, the Savior gave a sample prayer. This prayer is not to be recited for that would be considered vain repetitions. But the Lord provided a form or an example the leaders of his kingdom were to follow. Once again, the Savior is teaching principles. Thus, each prayer a leader utters should include these areas. First, each prayer is addressed to the Father, the creator of all. It provides an acknowledgment of his divine parentage and reverences his name.

The next portion of the prayer is also an acknowledgment of God's goodness to man. It is important that leaders maintain order through obedience to the commandments. By their obedience they show the desire to subordinate their own will to that of God. Once again, a feigned or forced obedience is not enough. Obedience can only be a free will offering.

In a prayer, items needed should also be requested. The Father is aware of individual needs as well as the concern regarding a leader's , but agency demands that the blessing be requested. As one asks for needs such as food and clothing or assistance in the life of an individual, the petitioner is reminded that God is the Master Giver and is deserving of our gratitude.

Next in the sample prayer, the Lord discusses forgiveness. This is a reminder that all men but Christ have sinned and must seek forgiveness. Not only should a leader be diligent in seeking forgiveness from God and man for their own errors, but he or she should forgive those who have been the source of injury.

Through the sample prayer, Christ indicates that temptations to disobey God's commandments are ever present in this mortal existence. As a counterbalance to the forces that seek the destruction of God's children, it is promised that an individual will not be tempted beyond that person's ability to resist. Thus, man's agency is maintained. This protection, however, is not extended to those people who are susceptible to a particular sin and frequent places where that sin is prominent. By choosing to enter those places or engaging in those practices, the individual rejects God's protection and assistance.

The last phrase in the prayer recognizes God as the supreme overlord of this world and all contained therein and thereon. It also confirms to the Father what had been said previously.

For the first ideal, Christ discussed the giving of alms and the need for pure charity. Prior to and during his ministry on both continents, powerful and wealthy people would contribute large sums of money to the poor in ostentatious displays. These contributions were not made out of concern for those in need but were made to enhance the donor's image among the public. Christ taught his disciples, those who would lead his kingdom in his absence, that the intent of the gift was more important than the amount. Those who gave to further their career or political standing or to receive the acclaim of man would have their reward from what men could or would give. Although these rewards might seem significant, at the time they pale into insignificance when compared with the gifts of the Spirit. In order to be filled with the Holy Ghost, an individual must give assistance to those in need with the proper intent. They do not seek acclaim or pomp and circumstance, but their desire is for the welfare of their brothers and sisters.

It is not possible to hide anything from the Father who knows and sees all, even the intent of a heart. The Savior's instructions are to provide the needed assistance in secret. Although the giving may be in secret, God will reward his servants openly and fill them with the Holy Ghost.

Christ's purpose in this beatitude with its ideals is to encourage the conversion of his disciples and establish the "life of the soul" as Elder Neal A. Maxwell has said. Not only does a true conversion exalt the individual, but it helps leaders assist those in their stewardship. They are filled with the Holy Spirit. Elder Maxwell said,

> When pondering "the life of the soul," it helps to strive for our own full conversion whereas the gospel seed first falls on "good ground"—which is defined by Jesus as those with an "honest and good heart" (Luke 8:15). Sequentially, such an individual "heareth," (Matthew 13:20, 23; JST Matthew 13:21; Matthew 5:6). It is "a mighty change" (Mosiah 5:2). Conversion basically represent the transformation from the "natural man" to becoming the "man of Christ" (Mosiah 3:19; Helaman 3:29; see also 2 Corinthians 5:17). It is a labor that takes more than an afternoon.
>
> The outcomes of this ongoing process include having "no more disposition to do evil, but to do good continually" (Mosiah 5:2). No wonder, therefore, this process enables those so converted to "strengthen [their] brethren" (Luke 22:32) and so lift others by being "ready always to give an answer to every man that asketh you a reason of the hope that is in you" (1 Peter 3:15)." (*Ensign*, May 2003, p. 70)

BLESSED ARE THE MEEK

Blessed are the meek: for they shall inherit the earth. (Matthew 5:5)

God desires for his children to become like him, and he continues the cycle of exaltation to accomplish that goal. A vital part in that process involves the wise use of agency. Agency is the vehicle which allows his children to be free to learn and experience and to choose to be like God. Nephi taught that all men "are free to choose liberty and eternal life . . . or to choose captivity and death, according to the captivity and power of the devil" (see 2 Nephi 2:27). Elder Neal A. Maxwell taught that "agency is essential to perfectibility, and meekness is essential to the wise use of agency—and to our recovery when we have misused our agency" (see Neal A. Maxwell, *Ensign*, March 1983). As he taught the future readers of his abridgement about faith and hope, the prophet Moroni wrote that one "cannot have faith and hope, save he be meek and lowly of heart." For none are "acceptable before God, save the meek and lowly in heart" (see Moroni 7:43-44). Thus, developing the attribute of being meek is essential for one's exaltation.

But does our definition for this attribute of meekness match its importance. Moses, the prophet who called plagues down on Egypt and led the righteous against those who worshipped the golden calf, is an example of being meek. He was considered "very meek, above all the men which were upon the face of the earth" (see Numbers 12:3). Another example comes from the Savior himself where he was considered meek and lowly in heart (see Matthew 11:29).

The examples cited in the scriptures above indicate there is more to being meek than in being kind and gentle and humble and more than exercising restraint. "It is the presentation of self in a posture of kindness and gentleness, reflecting certitude, strength, serenity, and a healthy self-esteem and self-control" (see Neal A Maxwell, *Ensign*, March 1983). Using this definition, it can be seen how the meek are less easily offended and less likely to give offense. Elder Maxwell continued his explanation of meekness. He said,

> Actually, meekness is not an attribute which is essential only in itself, said Moroni. It is also vital because one cannot develop those other crucial virtues—faith, hope and charity—without meekness. In the ecology of the eternal attributes, these cardinal characteristics are inextricably bound up together. Among them, meekness is often the initiator, facilitator, and consolidator. (Neal A. Maxwell, *Ensign*, March 1983)

This attribute is important for a leader in Christ's Church because

> the meek are able with regularity to peel off the encrustations of ego that form on one's soul so relentlessly and persistently, like barnacles on a ship. The meek are thus able to avoid the abuse of authority and power—a tendency to which, the Lord declared, "almost all" succumb. Except the meek. The

meek use power and authority properly, no doubt because their gentleness and meekness reflect a love unfeigned, a genuine caring. The influence they exercise flows from a deep concern. (Neal A. Maxwell, *Ensign*, March 1983)

In an article for the *Ensign*, Elder Robert E. Wells of the First Quorum of the Seventy (*an administrative organization*) used a story to illustrate the concept of being meek. While in Argentina, he visited a large ranch where a thousand head of horses were being raised and trained. Some of the horses were to be used by the nation's gauchos, but most were thoroughbred polo ponies, trained in Argentina and sold throughout the world. As he toured the ranch, Elder Wells wondered if he was going to see a rodeo where the horses were "broke" like the American cowboys do. The owner was aghast. "Not at this ranch you won't" was his emphatic answer. "Although a polo pony has to be obedient, lightning fast, fearless, and superbly maneuverable, we would never 'break' a horse—we don't want to break his spirit. We love our horses and work patiently with them until they are meek or *manso*. Our *manso* horses are still full of fire and spirit; but they are obedient and well trained."

Elder Wells saw a great application from this example for the meaning of *manso*, the Spanish word for meek. He taught that "the Savior didn't mean for us to be 'doormats'—he meant that we should be obedient and well trained. We can be strong, enthusiastic, talented, spirited, zealous, and still be 'meek'—able to coexist in the success-oriented world in which we live" (Robert E. Wells, *Ensign*, December 1987).

As Elder Maxwell taught, meekness is essential for the wise use of agency, which is essential for perfectibility. Thus, the blessing for developing meekness is that those who do so will inherit the earth. These are God's children who merit the celestial kingdom. These are

> they that are wise and have received the truth, and have taken the Holy Spirit for their guide, and have not been deceived—verily I say unto you, they shall not be hewn down and cast into the fire, but shall abide the day.
>
> And the earth shall be given unto them for an inheritance; and they shall multiply and wax strong, and their children shall grow up without sin unto salvation. (Doctrine and Covenants 45:57–58; see also Doctrine and Covenants 88:17–18)

Thus, it is easy to see why Christ stressed this attribute to his early disciples in their training. Leaders who are truly meek have received the truth of the gospel and have brought their own lives into compliance with God's will. In addition, meekness assists in the development of faith, hope, and charity in their lives. Meek leaders are well trained, yet they can be strong enough to maintain the purity of the ordinances and doctrines of the kingdom. They avoid the love and abuse of power in favor of the love for God's children. The ideals Christ associates with this beatitude are true wealth, spiritual light, divided loyalties, and strength of faith. Each allows an individual the opportunity to submit their will to that of the Father.

True Wealth

The first ideal regarding this beatitude deals with recognizing true wealth. Christ taught his disciples on both continents to

> lay not up for yourselves treasures upon earth, where moth and rust doth corrupt, and where thieves break through and steal:
>
> But lay up for yourselves treasures in heaven, where neither moth nor rust doth corrupt, and where thieves do not break through nor steal:

For where your treasure is, there will your heart be also.
(Matthew 6:19–21; see also 3 Nephi 13:19–21)

During mortality, an individual is expected to work and struggle to provide for the necessities of life. As Adam was being expelled from the Garden of Eden, the Lord told him that by "the sweat of thy face shalt thou eat bread" (see Genesis 3:19). Lucifer has taken that command and twisted it. Through the centuries since Adam, some of God's children have succumbed to the temptation to amass as much wealth as possible. The acquisition of material wealth can be taken to the point where all else is ignored. Those items that have eternal value are sacrificed for those that are transitory.

Lucifer even tried this approach as he tempted the Savior. Prior to delivering the Sermon on the Mount, Christ went into the wilderness to commune with God. After fasting for forty days and nights, the Savior was tempted by Satan with physical appetites, self-doubt, and wealth. In the last, Lucifer offered all the kingdoms of the world and all their glory if Christ would worship him instead of God. Christ refused, saying, "Thou shalt worship the Lord thy God, and him only shalt thou serve" (see Matthew 4:1–10). The Savior chose to treasure eternal wealth.

In this training, the Savior cautioned his disciples against sacrificing that which has eternal value for that which is transitory. True wealth lies not in metals or cloth; these items can tarnish, rot, or be stolen. True wealth lies in a testimony of the gospel and an eternal family. Seeking after the wealth and glory of the world for the sake of wealth and glory rejects God and his gospel. In a sense, the world replaces God as the item being worshipped. Thus, Saints are encouraged to "not spend money for that which is of no worth, nor your labor for that which cannot satisfy" (see 2 Nephi 9:51). Actions show what is valued, what is treasured.

The Sermon on the Mount was directed to leaders who would be serving the Lord full time and had to focus on directing and building up the kingdom of God. But not all leaders are Apostles or General Authorities. There are bishops and stake and quorum presidents, as well as auxiliary heads. They must seek for God's kingdom while providing for their families.

In a general epistle to the members of the Church in his day, Peter, the Chief Apostle, wrote of the value of an individual's testimony. He said,

> That the trial of your faith, being much more precious than of gold that perisheth, though it be tried with fire, might be found unto praise and honor and glory at the appearing of Jesus Christ. (1 Peter 1:7)

The principle being taught in this beatitude is that a testimony of Christ and his gospel is of the highest value. The obtaining and strengthening of that testimony should not be sacrificed for money, work, or leisure. James Talmage wrote,

> Many there were and many there are whose principal effort in life has been that of amassing treasures of earth, the mere possession of which entails responsibility, care, and disturbing anxiety. Some kinds of wealth are endangered by the ravages of moth, such as silks and velvets, satins and furs; some are destroyed by corrosion and rust—silver and copper and steel; while these and others are not infrequently made the booty of thieves. Infinitely more precious are the treasures of a life well spent, the wealth of good deeds, the account of which is kept in heaven, where the riches of righteous

achievement are safe from moth, rust and robbers. (*Jesus the Christ*, p. 242)

Thus, a leader in Christ's Church should recognize that which has real value and focus on the crucial tasks that leads to that treasure. This is not to say a leader is to live in abject poverty. Money or material wealth is often needed to advance the work of the kingdom. But this kind of wealth should not be the treasure of one's life.

Hundreds of years before Christ's mortal ministry, Jacob taught his people in the Americas that

> before ye seek for riches, seek ye for the Kingdom of God.
>
> And after ye have obtained a hope in Christ ye shall obtain riches, if ye seek them; and ye will seek them for the intent to do good—to clothe the naked, and to feed the hungry, and to liberate the captive, and administer relief to the sick and afflicted. (Jacob 2:18–19)

The counsel from a prophet of God is to first seek to obtain a testimony, "a hope in Christ." Then, if wealth is desired, the individual will seek riches with the intent to aid in Christ's work. This exhibits a charitable rather than a covetous nature.

While Christ was teaching a large number of people, a man approached to ask for the Savior's intervention. This man's brother, the eldest son in the family and lawfully the inheritor of all his father had, was refusing to divide the inheritance with his younger brother. Perhaps sensing a covetous nature, the Savior warned, "Take heed, and beware of covetousness: for a man's life consisteth not in the abundance of the things which he possesseth" (see Luke 12:13–15). To illustrate his point further, the Savior taught a parable:

> The ground of a certain rich man brought forth plentifully:
>
> And he thought within himself, saying, What shall I do, because I have no room where to bestow my fruits?
>
> And he said, This will I do: I will pull down my barns, and build greater; and there will I bestow all my fruits and my goods.
>
> And I will say to my soul, Soul, thou hast much goods laid up for many years; take thine ease, eat, drink and be merry.
>
> But God said unto him, Thou fool, this night thy soul shall be required of thee: then whose shall those things be, which thou hast provided?
>
> So is he that layeth up treasure for himself, and is not rich toward God. (Luke 12:16–21)

This parable reiterates the Savior's teachings from the Sermon on the Mount. Any individual who does not seek true wealth—a hope in Christ—is a fool. No amount of gold, silver, land, horses, or any kind of treasure will benefit one at the judgment seat of Christ. At another time, the Savior asked,

> For what is a man profited, if he shall gain the whole world, and lose his own soul? Or what shall a man give in exchange for his soul? (Matthew 16:26)

The Savior's teachings regarding true wealth were not limited to material possessions. The concept of what consists as false wealth can be extended to occupations, hobbies, and so forth. Anything that draws an individual from Christ is false wealth. During one of his journeys, Christ came to a certain village and met a woman named Martha, who invited him to her home so he could teach. As Christ taught inside the house, Martha was "cumbered about much serving," providing for those who were in attendance. In that same household was Martha's sister, Mary. Instead of assisting her sister with the chores in serving their guests, Mary sat at the Master's feet and listened. This bothered Martha and she asked the Savior to remind her sister of her responsibilities as a hostess. Instead of a reprimand for Mary, the Savior said,

> Martha, Martha, thou art careful and troubled about many things:
>
> But one thing is needful: and Mary hath chosen that good part, which shall not be taken away from her. (Luke 10: 41–42)

In order to inherit the earth or, in other words, to enter the celestial kingdom, an individual must have the proper priorities. This is truer for a leader in Christ's Church. The proper focus, the better part, is to seek after the true wealth found in the gospel. "For where your treasure is, there will be your heart also."

Spiritual Light

In gospel usage, light is often used as a synonym for truth and goodness while darkness is used to describe falsehood and evil. The Psalmist wrote that "God is the Lord, which hath shewed us the light" (see Psalms 118:27). At the birth of his son who would become the prophet to prepare the way for the Messiah, Zacharias prophesied that John would "give light to them that sit in darkness" (see Luke 1:79). Those who follow the gospel are considered the "children of light" (see 1 Thessalonians 5:5).

Bruce McConkie provides an understanding of this concept in *Mormon Doctrine*. He wrote,

> Gospel light is the mental and spiritual enlightenment from God which enables men to receive truth and gain salvation. Light is an attribute of Deity and shines forth from him; in him it is found in its fullness and perfection. (*Mormon Doctrine*, p. 444)

In this next ideal for those who are or seek to be meek, the Savior taught the disciples about spiritual light. He said,

> The light of the body is the eye: if therefore thine eye be single to the glory of God, thy whole body shall be full of light.
>
> But if thine eye be evil, thy whole body shall be full of darkness. If therefore the light that is in thee be darkness, how great is that darkness! (Matthew 6:22–23; see also 3 Nephi 13: 22–23)

In these instructions, the Savior was addressing his disciples, those whom he had chosen, who

> had received the light of God; the degree of belief they had already professed was proof of that. Should they turn from the great emprice on which they had embarked, the light would be lost, and the succeeding darkness would be denser that that from which they had been relieved. (*Jesus the Christ*, p. 243)

The verses of the Savior's teachings regarding spiritual light are reminiscent of the beatitude on persecution. In that beatitude, the disciples were encouraged to hold Christ and the gospel up for the world to see.

Bruce McConkie wrote,

> A light that is hidden, whose guiding rays are covered by a bushel, is of no value to one stumbling in darkness. Similarly, the true saints must let the gospel light shine forth from them to all men, lest the saints, as the hidden candle, fail to fulfill their purpose in life. (DNTC, p. 240)

For an individual to see, the eyes must focus light. It is eyesight that allows for many vital processes to occur. The Savior directs the leaders of his kingdom to be single or to focus on living the commandments and advancing the kingdom. By doing so in the prescribed manner, that individual would be full of light or, in other words, be full of mental and spiritual enlightenment from God. Thus, the kingdom of God is advanced. But if a leader chooses evil, that enlightenment is withdrawn. That individual is left alone, without the aid of the Holy Ghost. Some even become antagonistic toward the Church (refer to Doctrine and Covenants 121:34–38).

Besides focusing on the work, James Talmage provides an added dimension. In *Jesus the Christ*, he wrote,

> Spiritual light is shown to be greater than any product of physical illuminants. What does the brightest light avail the man who is blind? It is the bodily eye that discerns the light of the candle, the lamp of the sun; and the spiritual eye sees by spiritual light; if then man's spiritual eye be single, that is, pure and undimmed by sin, he is filled with the light that shall show him the way to God; whereas if his soul's eye be evil, he will be as one full of darkness. Solemn caution is expressed in the summary. "If therefore the light that is

in thee be darkness, how great is that darkness!" (*Jesus the Christ*, p. 243)

In a separate version of teaching spiritual light, Luke added a metaphor. He wrote,

> No man, when he hath lighted a candle, putteth it in a secret place, neither under a bushel, but on a candlestick, that they which come in may see the light.
>
> The light of the body is the eye: therefore when thine eye is single, thy whole body also is full of light; but when thine eye is evil, thy body is also full of darkness.
>
> Take heed therefore that the light which is in thee be not darkness.
>
> If thy whole body therefore be full of light, having no part dark, the whole shall be full of light, as when the bright shining of a candle doth give thee light. (Luke 11:33–36)

In modern days, the Lord told the Prophet Joseph Smith,

> And if your eye be single to my glory, your whole bodies shall be filled with light, and there shall be no darkness in you; and that body which is filled with light comprehendeth all things.
>
> Therefore, sanctify yourselves that your minds become single to God, and the days will come that you shall see him; for he will unveil his face unto you, and it shall be in his own time, and in his own way, and according to his own will. (Doctrine and Covenants 88:67–68)

In order to see clearly, the physical eye must be free of imperfections. The lens, pupil, rods, and cones must all function properly. If not, an individual will not be able to focus properly and see. This also happens in a spiritual sense. Sin closes one's sensitivity to direction from the Holy Ghost. Their light becomes dark. As a leader focuses on the things of the gospel and works to be clean from sin, where the eye is single, he or she will be able to comprehend items of import. The Spirit of the Lord will reveal what is necessary to improve their life or magnify their calling.

But the Savior warns, "Take heed, therefore that the light which is in thee be not darkness." If an individual does not seek God's glory, does not purge sin from their lives the Holy Ghost is driven away and there is no light, only darkness. "For of him unto whom much is given much is required; and he who sins against the greater light shall receive the greater condemnation" (see Doctrine and Covenants 82:3; see also Alma 9:23; 45:12). The leader is left under the influence of Satan.

Divided Loyalties

So far, in his instructions regarding meekness, the Savior has taught his disciples about seeking true wealth and concentrating on being sanctified that their mind would be single to God's purpose. Both of these ideals stress the need for a leader of Christ's Church to focus on those items that have eternal worth. This next ideal continues with that theme. The Savior reminded his disciples that

> no man can serve two masters: for either he will hate the one, and love the other; or else he will hold to the one, and despise the other. Ye cannot serve God and Mammon. (Matthew 6:24; see also 3 Nephi 13:24)

In order to be meek, the leaders of Christ's Church cannot be divided in their loyalties. The doctrines, philosophies, and practices of the world change often and cannot achieve God's purpose of exalting God's children. It is not possible for a leader to serve effectively in his or her call and also adhere to worldly doctrines. James taught "that the friendship of the world is enmity with god" and that "whosoever . . . will be a friend of the world is the enemy of God" (see James 4:4). Thus, a leader who attempts to serve two masters "will hate the one and love the other; or else he will hold to the one, and despise the other." This is because the best and highest the world produces cannot exalt a single individual. Anything diverting effort from that which exalts is opposing the Father.

In more recent times, Brigham Young explains that those

> who love and serve God with all their hearts rejoice evermore, pray without ceasing, and in everything give thanks; but they who try to serve God and still cling to the spirit of the world, have got on two yokes—the yoke of Jesus and the yoke of the devil, and they will have plenty to do. They will have a warfare inside and outside, and the labor will be galling, for they are directly in opposition one to the other. Cast off the yoke of the enemy, and put on the yoke of Christ, and you will say that his yoke is easy and his burden is light. (Brigham Young as quoted by Robert Millet in *The Call to Discipleship*)

Thus, no man can serve two masters. If an attempt is made to accommodate both God and Satan, there will be inner and external turmoil. The individual will not be able to focus on their labors as they should and the work of exalting God's children will suffer.

Strength of Faith

For the last ideal in this beatitude, the Lord turns to discussing a leader's strength of faith. In Palestine, he begins this portion of his training by reiterating the Apostles mission call:

> And, again, I say unto you, go ye into the world, and care not for the world; for the world will hate you, and will persecute you, and will turn you out of their synagogues. (Matthew 6:25 JST)

The Savior reminds his disciples of their call to take the gospel to the world. In fulfilling this assignment, in teaching the gospel in its pure, exalting form, and while maintaining the ordinances as prescribed, there would be persecution. Christ's disciples would be hated and turned out of synagogues or excommunicated from mainstream society. Now as well as then, Church leaders are to disregard the superfluous and take the gospel to the world.

Christ continued his instructions:

> Nevertheless, ye shall go from house to house, teaching the people; and I will go before you.
>
> And your heavenly Father will provide for you whatsoever things ye need for food, what ye shall eat; and for raiment, what ye shall wear or put on. (Matthew 6:26–27 JST)

For many leaders in Christ's Church, the command to provide for their own maintenance and that of their family is very important (see 1 Timothy 5:8; Doctrine and Covenants 75:28). Bruce McConkie wrote that "work, industry, frugality—sowing, reaping and eating our bread by the sweat of our faces—such is the royal order of life. From the beginning men have been commanded to labor in seed time and harvest and to lay up in store against times of winter and famine" (*The Mortal Messiah* 2:156)

Those who have been called by the Lord to serve in a full-time capacity such as General Authorities and missionaries are exempt from this requirement. They are to concentrate on building up the kingdom of God. "For the Lord will provide whatsoever things ye need." The Lord's disciples

> are to forsake worldly pursuits—their fishing boats, the customs house, their fields and vineyards, all temporal enterprises—and use all their time, talents and means for the building up of the earthly kingdom and the establishment of the cause of Christianity. Others also, the seventies among them, will tread a like path in due course. The Lord's missionaries and ministers engage in such important labors that no worldly pursuit can be permitted to interfere; nothing pertaining to this world can be allowed to dilute and divide the energy and strength of the Lords' servants. (*The Mortal Messiah* 2:155)

Once again there is a difference in the instructions given to the American and Palestinian disciples. In the Americas, prior to this time, Christ had been addressing the crowd that had gathered by the temple in the land Bountiful. At this point, the Savior turned to address only the American disciples.

> And now it came to pass that when Jesus had spoken these words he looked upon the twelve whom he had chosen, and said unto them: Remember the words which I have spoken. For behold, ye are they whom I have chosen to minister unto this people. Therefore I say unto you, take no thought for your life, what ye shall eat, or what ye shall drink; nor yet for your body, what ye shall put on. Is not the life more than meat, and the body more than raiment? (3 Nephi 13:25)

After reminding his American leaders that he had chosen them as ministers for the people, Christ echoed an item that had been taught to the Palestinian apostles in an earlier beatitude. The disciples are to focus on the eternal matters of the gospel. Christ points out that life is more than eating and there is more to the body than worrying about clothing: "Shall we concern ourselves with life itself—the life of the body and the life of the soul—or merely with the food we eat and the rags or robes we chance to use as covering raiment?" (*The Mortal Messiah* 2:157).

Christ continued,

> Behold the fowls of the air: for they sow not, neither do they reap, nor gather into barns; yet your heavenly Father feedeth them. Are ye not much better than they?
>
> Which of you by taking thought can add one cubit unto his stature?
>
> And why take ye thought for raiment? Consider the lilies of the field, how they grow; they toil not, neither do they spin:
>
> And yet I say unto you, That even Solomon in all his glory was not arrayed like one of these.
>
> Wherefore, if God so clothe the grass of the field, which today is, and tomorrow is cast into the oven, how much more will he not provide for you, if ye are not of little faith.
>
> Therefore take no thought, saying, What shall we eat? Or, What shall we drink? Or, Wherewithal shall we be clothed?
>
> (For after all these things do the Gentiles seek:) for your heavenly Father knoweth that ye have need of all these things. (Matthew 6:26–32; see also 3 Nephi 13:26–32)

While the general body of the Church is expected to be self-reliant, to provide for themselves and their families, those who serve full time are different. Those who serve in this capacity are to focus on their assignment. They are to have

> no concern about business enterprises or temporal pursuits. They are to be free of the encumbering obligations that always attend those who manage temporal affairs. Their whole attention and all of their strengths and talents are to be centered on the work of the ministry. And they have the Father's promise that he will look after their daily needs. (DNTC 1:243)

After all the fowls of the air are fed without having to sow, reap, or gather into barns, nor do the lilies of the field grow, toil, or spin cloth, yet they are considered more beautiful than Solomon in all his glory. The fowls of the air and lilies of the field are considered important in the Lord's eyes but not as important as his children. Thus, relying on the Lord for the necessities of life requires a leader to exhibit his or her strength of faith.

The Savior concluded this ideal by saying,

> Wherefore, seek not the things of this world but seek ye first to build up the Kingdom of God, and to establish his righteousness; and all these things shall be added unto you.
>
> Take therefore no thought for the morrow: for the morrow shall take thought for the things of itself. Sufficient unto the day is the evil thereof. (Matthew 6:33–34)

In the Americas, the Savior said,

But seek ye first the Kingdom of God and his righteousness, and all these things shall be added unto you.

Take therefore no thought for the morrow, for the morrow shall take thought for the things of itself. Sufficient is the day unto the evil thereof. (3 Nephi 13:33–34)

In both portions of the world, the Savior counseled the leaders of his Church to focus their efforts on building up the kingdom of God rather than desiring the things of the world. This is another reminder to ignore that which is transitory and concentrate on the eternal. The priorities for a Church leader is to concentrate first on their call to establish God's kingdom. If a leader does this, then the leader shall be clothed, fed, and housed as needed.

Concentrating on the kingdom rather than on seeking wealth or providing the necessities of life requires great faith in the Savior. This was more evident at the time when Christ taught his disciples than now. But he has promised that those items which are needed will be "added unto you." Since the Lord provides beauty in lilies of the field, food for the fowls of the air, and raiment for the grass, "how much more will he provide for you?"

Summary

It is natural for a person to be concerned about the necessities of life, including food, clothing, and shelter. The Lord expects an individual to be self-reliant and to provide for the needs of his or her family. A leader in Christ's Church has a different focus. Those who do not serve full time must find a balance between their occupation and family and Church service. A General Authority with a full-time call must eschew worldly affairs to oversee the growth and well-being of God's kingdom on earth.

In both instances, a leader must go forward in his or her call, trusting in the Father. If God can provide for the fowls of the air and adorn the lilies of the field, he can sustain his chosen servants. Thus, the servants are to go into the world, taking the gospel message to God's children. The Savior's instructions are that they are not to care for the wealth or opinions or attitudes of the world but to teach Christ's message in its pure form. As they do so, hatred and persecution will follow, for Satan will not allow the work to go forward unhindered. Nevertheless, as leaders go about their responsibilities, teaching the people, God will be with them and provide for the necessities of life.

Another ideal discussed in this beatitude refers to the problem of divided loyalties. The Savior taught that a leader cannot have a strong testimony of the gospel and Christ and cannot effectively further God's Kingdom while also believing in the philosophies of the world, which come from Satan. The objectives of each are in direct opposition to the other. Christ seeks to provide the opportunity for God's children to obtain their exaltation. Lucifer would use his brothers and sisters in an attempt to supplant the Father. With these opposing goals, a leader or individual with feet in both camps will "hate the one and love the other." A leader in Christ's kingdom must serve wholeheartedly. There is enough conflict in life without having inner turmoil.

In this beatitude, the Savior also discussed the importance of seeking after gospel truth. Knowledge is important but the leaders of Christ's Church are expected to know and have a firm testimony of the doctrines of the kingdom. This is particularly important since a leader's charge is to maintain the doctrines in their pure, exalting form. In addition, a knowledge of the commandments is necessary for an individual to purge his or her life of sin and be obedient to God's commandments. A caution is included for those who would turn from the light and not repent. That light, the truth and joy, which was present in the leader at one time would be replaced with darkness and the falsehoods of Lucifer, an opposite of that enjoyed before.

The first ideal taught regarding this beatitude encourages leaders to seek after true wealth. True wealth is not found in amassing precious metals, clothing, or things, or items that tarnish, rot, or are stolen. True wealth is that which remains with the individual when he or she progresses into the next realm. The true wealth of an individual is a life well lived, full-hearted obedience to the gospel, and a strong and vibrant testimony of Christ, his kingdom, and his teachings.

The ideals of seeking after true wealth, keeping one's eye single to God's glory, taking care to serve only God rather than the adversary, and developing strength in one's faith helps a leader be meek. Those who do so are obedient to God's commandments and focused in developing a contrite spirit and a humble heart. They are strong, enthusiastic, talented, spirited, zealous, obedient, well trained—meek. The promised blessing for this type of person is to inherit the earth, a blessing reserved for those in the highest degree of the celestial kingdom.

BLESSED ARE THEY THAT MOURN

Blessed are they that mourn: for they shall be comforted. (Matthew 5:4)

This beatitude seems a little odd: those who mourn are blessed. It seems to imply that suffering is a desirable state and contradicts Lehi's teaching that "men are, that they might have joy" (see 2 Nephi 2:25). In this portion of the Sermon on the Mount, the Savior resolves this misunderstanding. He wants the Church taught that an individual is not blessed because of their sorrow rather they are blessed because of what they do to be comforted.

As a perfect, immortal being, God lives in perfect joy. Because of his love for us, his children, he has put in place a plan the enables us to become perfect like him and participate in that joy. It was mentioned in a prior beatitude that agency is essential for perfectibility, and an operative feature for agency involves opposites. A person chooses between right and wrong, happiness or pain, life or death. By distilling the alternatives of a decision to their essence, looking at the consequences of each alternative, one often finds the choices are between happiness and sorrow.

Thus, if an individual desires a blessing or to feel joy, he or she must obey the law upon which the blessing is based (see Doctrine and Covenants 130:20-21). But if the person disobeys, there is a punishment affixed which is the opposite of the blessing (see Alma 42:16). Nephi taught,

> Wherefore, the ends of the law which the Holy One hath given, unto the inflicting of the punishment which is affixed, which punishment that is affixed is in opposition to that of the happiness which is affixed, to answer the ends of the atonement—
>
> For it must needs be, that there is an opposition in all things. (2 Nephi 2:10-11)

Obedience to God's commandments brings about joy. It is a natural consequence. If an individual chooses to disobey a commandment, they can expect to feel sorrow "in opposition to that happiness which is affixed." Compliance with the Word of Wisdom (*a health code for Latter-day Saints*) brings health, strength, and wisdom, blessings which contribute to happiness. Those who break this law of health can expect illness instead of health, weakness instead of strength, and foolishness instead of wisdom. Disobedience to the other commandments of God brings similar results. In addition to the sorrow that results from experiencing the natural consequences of disobedience, there is an alienation from God and things of righteousness (see Helaman 14:18). This alienation from God is a spiritual death and brings its own sorrow. Thus, one cause of sorrow and mourning is sin.

Another source of sorrow is that of physical death. Enoch taught that because of Adam's fall came death and Adam's descendants are made partakers of misery and woe (see Moses 6:48). Sorrow often comes from the idea that those we have loved have ceased to exist. They are no more.

There is also a fear that we as individuals will cease to be after a lifetime of accumulating knowledge and experience.

In completing the Atonement, the Savior addressed the two major causes of mourning mentioned: physical and spiritual death.

Just prior to being taken into custody by the Romans, the Savior went to the Garden of Gethsemane on the Mount of Olives where he could pray and receive strength. It was during those few moments of solitude that Jesus Christ atoned for the sins of those who would repent (see Luke 22:39–46). The method of how this was accomplished has not been revealed. But it was accomplished. Paul, a beneficiary of this blessing, told the Hebrew Saints that "Christ was once offered to bear the sins of many" (see Hebrews 9:28). This remission of sins is extended to all but accepted by few. Jacob, the brother of Nephi, taught that

> redemption cometh in and through the Holy Messiah; for he is full of grace and truth.
>
> Behold, he offereth himself a sacrifice for sin, to answer the ends of the law, unto all those who have a broken heart and a contrite spirit; and unto none else can the ends of the law be answered. (2 Nephi 2: 6–7)

The sorrows of sin, of spiritual death, were removed by the Savior, conditioned upon individual repentance. When repentance is complete, the sins are forgiven, the Lord remembers them no more, and joy returns (see Doctrine and Covenants 58:42). Those who elect to forego the repentance process continue to receive spiritual death as compensation (see Romans 6:23). They choose sorrow because they do not change their behavior.

Jesus Christ not only atoned for sin but also provided a victory over physical death. Death is not an annihilation of matter or an individual ceasing to exist. It is a change of status.

> This death consists in the separation of the eternal spirit from the mortal body so that the body is left to go back to the dust or element from which it was created (meaning organized), and the spirit is left to sojourn in a world of waiting spirits. (*Mormon Doctrine*, p. 185)

It is the spirit, a child of Heavenly Parents, that animates the body and accumulates knowledge and experience. Upon death, while the body is buried, the spirit continues to exist until the next portion of the plan of happiness occurs.

The reverse of death is called Resurrection. This is when the spirit is united with a perfect, immortal, physical body (see *Mormon Doctrine*, p. 637; see also Alma 11:43, 45). Christ was the first to be resurrected (see 1 Corinthians 15:23). While not present for the actual event, the fact of the Resurrection of Jesus was witnessed by Peter, the Apostles in Palestine, over five hundred more people in Palestine, and thousands of people in the land of Bountiful in the Americas.

Redemption from spiritual death is conditioned upon repentance, but there is no requirement to be met to be resurrected. It is universal, given to all freely. Alma taught that

> this restoration shall come to all, both old and young, both bond and free, both male and female, both the wicked and the righteous; and even there shall not so much as a hair of their heads be lost. (Alma 11:44; see also 1 Corinthians 15:22)

All mankind will be resurrected. In celebration of this universal event, Paul wrote to the Corinthians,

> For this corruptible must put on incorruption, and this mortal must put on immortality.

> So when this corruptible shall have put on incorruption, and this mortal shall put on immortality, then shall be brought to pass the saying that is written, Death is swallowed up in victory.
>
> O death, where is thy sting? O grave, where is thy victory?
>
> The sting of death is sin; and the strength of sin is the law.
>
> But thanks be to God, which giveth us the victory through our Lord Jesus Christ. (1 Corinthians 15:53–56)

Through the Savior, the major causes of mourning have been resolved. Remitting of sins is conditional. Those who desire this blessing can repent and forsake sin. If they do so, their sins are forgiven and forgotten. The source of sorrow is removed and happiness returns. The person is comforted. But the victory over death, the Resurrection, is universal. There is no permanent separation from loved ones. Nor is there the annihilation of self. Once again, comfort is provided.

In prior Beatitudes, the Savior taught his disciples what responses to expect from others and what standards of behavior Church leaders should follow. The last two Beatitudes are different. Christ now instructs the leaders of his Church what to teach the general membership of the Church regarding standards of conduct.

In order to receive comfort, those who mourn must conform to correct principles, as shown in repenting of sins. The ideals identified by the Savior to be taught to the Saints for this beatitude deal with eliminating contention between people, which is often the source of sorrow. These ideals involve judging others, hypocrisy, and keeping doctrines of the kingdom sacred.

Judging Others

> Now these are the words which Jesus taught his disciples that they should say unto the people. Judge not unrighteously, that ye be not judged: but judge righteous judgment. (Matthew 7:1 JST)

In the Americas, when he taught this ideal, Christ turned to the crowd so all could hear instead of restricting his comments to a few (see 3 Nephi 14:1). Yet on both continents, the message was the same: members of his Church were to be taught to avoid making unrighteous judgment.

These instructions should not be construed to mean judgments are to be avoided. Not making judgments is not feasible or wise. Each person must evaluate occupations, whom to date and marry, or those with whom to associate among many other areas. The key in this teaching is to make righteous judgments. Centuries earlier, the Lord told Moses,

> Ye shall do no unrighteousness in judgment: thou shalt not respect the person of the poor, nor honor the person of the mighty: but in righteousness thou shalt judge thy neighbor. (Leviticus 19:15)

On one occasion, when he was in the temple, the Savior responded to criticisms by saying, "Judge not according to your traditions, but judge righteous judgment" (John 7:24 JST). Bruce R. McConkie, in discussing the Savior's admonition about making judgments, said,

> This is not a prohibition against sitting in judgment either on ones fellowmen or upon principles of right and wrong, for the Saints are commanded to do those very things. The sense and meaning of our Lord's utterances is, "Condemn

not, that ye be not condemned." It is "Judge wisely and righteously, so that ye may be judged in like manner."

Judgment is one of the attributes of godliness which the saints are commanded to seek. (DNTC p. 245)

Inappropriate judgments, those given in a manner favoring one side over another in spite of the evidence or according to false traditions, is considered unrighteous judgment. This is often the cause of mourning for an individual. It creates contention between people.

This raises the question of what is considered righteous judgment or how one makes a righteous judgment. The last prophet of the Book of Mormon, Moroni, gave some guidelines and wrote,

For behold, my brethren, it is given unto you to judge, that ye may know good from evil; and the way to judge is as plain, that ye may know with a perfect knowledge, as the daylight is from the dark night.

> For behold, the Spirit of Christ is given to every man, that he may know good from evil; wherefore, I show unto you the way to judge; for every thing which inviteth to do good, and to persuade to believe in Christ, is sent forth by the power and gift of Christ; wherefore ye may know with a perfect knowledge it is of God.
>
> But whatsoever thing persuadeth men to do evil, and believe not in Christ, and deny him, and serve not God, then ye may know with a perfect knowledge it is of the devil; for after this manner doth the devil work, for he persuadeth no man to do good, no, not one; neither do his angels; neither do they who subject themselves unto him.
>
> And now, my brethren, seeing that ye know the light by which ye may judge, which light is the light of Christ, see

> that ye do not judge wrongfully; for with that same judgment which ye judge ye shall also be judged. (Moroni 7:15–18)

There are two principles provided by Moroni regarding judgment. The first involves the spirit of Christ (also referred to as the Light of Christ). All of God's children have received this gift that they might know good from evil. The Light of Christ, commonly known as a conscience, will prompt an individual to choose correctly. The second principle regarding judgment is to seek for the good and avoid that which is evil. That which teaches of Christ and righteousness is good. The opposite is not. At the end of his teaching regarding this principle, Moroni echoed Christ's warning given centuries earlier that a person would be judged in the same manner he judged others. Christ had instructed his disciples to teach the Saints that

> for with what judgment ye judge, ye shall be judged: and with what measure ye mete, it shall be measured to you again. (Matthew 7:2 see also 3 Nephi 14:2)

Using the same principle of reciprocation shown in forgiveness, the Savior indicates that the judge will be judged by the same standards and manner by which he judges. So, it is in each Saints' own best interest not to judge by false tradition, appearance, wealth, or standing in society but to judge righteously.

Spencer W. Kimball wrote that

> the Lord will judge with the same measurements meted out by us. If we are harsh, we should not expect other than harshness. If we are merciful with those who injure us, he will be merciful with us in our errors. If we are unforgiving, he will leave us weltering in our own sins. (*The Miracle of Forgiveness*, p. 267)

As the Saints conduct their daily business, judgments are required. One of the many responsibilities of a leader in Christ's Church is to help those in his or her stewardship learn to make wise judgments. Members are not to judge rashly or without proper and prayerful consideration. They are not to condemn one another. If unrighteous judgment occurs, it brings contention and is the cause of much sorrow. A Saint judges with the spirit of Christ. Brigham Young taught,

> Let no man judge his fellow being, unless he knows he has the mind of Christ within him. We ought to reflect seriously upon this point; how often it is said—"Such a person has done wrong, and he cannot be a Saint, or he would not do so." How do you know? We hear some swear and lie; they trample upon the rights of their neighbor, break the Sabbath by staying away from meeting, riding about the city, hunting horses and cattle, or working in the canyons. Do not judge such persons, for you do not know the design of the Lord concerning them; therefore do not say they are not Saints. What shall we do with them? Bear with them. The brethren and sisters from the old countries frequently place great confidence in the American Elders who have been their pastors, but some trifling thing occurs that does not appear right to them, and they say in a moment, "That Elder is not a Latter-day Saint." A person who would say another is not a Latter-day Saint, for some trifling affair in human life proves that he does not possess the Spirit of God. Think of this, brethren and sisters; write it down, that you may refresh your memories with it; carry it with you and look at if often. If I judge my brethren and sisters, unless I judge them by the revelations of Jesus Christ, I have not the

Spirit of Christ; if I had, I should judge no man. (*Discourses of Brigham Young*, p. 277–278)

In a book published under the direction of the First Presidency, the Saints are told,

> Sometimes people feel it is wrong to judge others in any way. While it is true that you should not condemn others or judge them unrighteously, you will need to make judgments of ideas, situations, and people throughout your life. The Lord has given many commandments that you cannot keep without making judgments. For example He has said: "Beware of false prophets. . . . Ye shall know them by their fruits" (Matthew 7:15-16) and "Go ye out from among the wicked" (D & C 38:42). You need to make judgments of people in many of your important decisions, such as choosing friends, voting for government leaders, and choosing an eternal companion.
>
> Your righteous judgments about others can provide needed guidance for them and, in some cases, protection for you and your family. Approach any such judgments with care and compassion. As much as you can, judge people's situations rather than judging the people themselves. Whenever possible, refrain from making judgments until you have an adequate knowledge of the facts. Always be sensitive to the Holy Spirit, who can guide your decisions. Remember Alma's counsel to his son, Corianton: "See that you are merciful unto your brethren; deal justly, judge righteously, and do good continually" (Alma 41:14). (*True to the Faith: A Gospel Reference*, p. 90–91)

Hypocrisy

> And again, ye shall say unto them, Why is it that thou beholdest the mote that is in thy brother's eye, but considerest not the beam that is in thine own eye?
>
> Or how wilt thou say to thy brother, let me pull out the mote out of thine eye; and canst not behold a beam in thine own eye? (Matthew 7:4–5 JST; see also 3 Nephi 14:3–4)

This second ideal expands upon the concept of judging righteously. A hypocrite dismisses or ignores their own sins yet desires to help someone else correct a minor fault. This is an example of exercising unrighteous judgment. The Saints of Christ's Church were to be counseled against this form of hypocrisy because of the resentment and contention it engenders.

In examining the metaphor used by the Savior, one understands that a mote is something small, of little or no consequence, while a beam is large and easily discerned. Christ's analogy is of an individual who has committed serious sin that is as visible as a beam in a house attempting to correct another individual who has a small or indiscernible fault of no eternal consequence. Spencer W. Kimball wrote,

> This should leave no doubt in any mind. The unequallness of the beam and the mote is telling. A mote is a tiny sliver like a small portion from a toothpick, while the beam is usually a great, strong timber or metal which runs from wall to wall to support the heavy roof of the building. When one is loaded down with beam-size weaknesses and sins, it is certainly wrong to forget his own difficult position while he makes mountains of the molehill-size errors of his brother.

> Our vision is completely obscured when we have no mirror to hold up to our own faults and look only for the foibles of others. When we follow the instructions of the Lord, we are kept so busy perfecting ourselves that we come to realize that the faults of others are small in comparison. We should establish the delightful habit, then, of minimizing the weaknesses of others and thus increase our own virtues. (*The Miracle of Forgiveness*, p. 269)

After teaching the principle, Christ gives his Palestinian Apostles an example.

> And Jesus said unto his disciples, Beholdest thou the Scribes, and the Pharisees, and the Priests, and the Levites? They teach in their synagogues, but do not observe the law, nor the commandments; and all have gone out of the way, and are under sin.
>
> Go thou and say unto them, Why teach ye men the law and the commandments, when ye yourselves are the children of corruption?
>
> Say unto them, Ye hypocrites, first cast out the beam out of thine own eye; and then shalt Thou see clearly to cast out the mote out of they brother's eye. (Matthew 7:6–8 JST; see also 3 Nephi 14:5)

The Savior condemned the religious leaders of Israel for hypocrisy. They taught and required others to live the Law of Moses and the commandments of God while they failed to observe their own teachings.

In Palestine and the New World, the Saints were taught to make sure their own lives were clean of sin before seeking to correct others. When that has been accomplished, the individual will see more clearly if there is any need to correct another.

Keeping Doctrines Sacred

In the book *Mormon Doctrine*, a mystery is defined as

> something which cannot be explained, either because it is beyond human comprehension in general, or because some particular man has not learned enough to understand it. Accordingly, some matters of doctrine, philosophy, or science may be a mystery to one person and not to another. When a thing is understood it is no longer a mystery. In the eternal sense there are no mysteries; all things are known to and understood by Deity; and there will be no mysteries among exalted beings, for they too shall know all things. (*Mormon Doctrine*, p. 523)

The *Bible Dictionary* explains that a mystery is "a spiritual truth that was once hidden but now is revealed and that, without special revelation, would have remained unknown" (*Bible Dictionary*, p. 736).

By these definitions, it is shown that a mystery is not something unknowable; it is just unknown at the present to a person or a people. It is not intended that these items of doctrine or mysteries remain unrevealed throughout the eternities for, as mentioned by Bruce R. McConkie, all knowledge will be held by exalted beings. Receipt of the knowledge of mysteries can be obtained during mortality or after. But it is the responsibility of the individual to seek for the desired understanding.

The scriptures teach that those who repent of their sins, exercise faith in Christ, obey the commandments, and ask shall receive knowledge of the mysteries by revelation (see Alma 26:22; Doctrine and Covenants

42:61). This search to understand the mysteries is not hypothetical. Abraham sought to possess greater knowledge and received the blessings and doctrines of the priesthood, including the covenants of exaltation (see Abraham 1:2; 2:9–11). When he was young, Nephi sought to understand the teachings of his father, which were mysteries to the youth. His prayers were answered and the knowledge he sought was revealed in vision (see 1 Nephi 11). During his mortal ministry, Christ taught his disciples "things which have been kept secret from the foundations of the world" (see Matthew 13:35). He taught mysteries—spiritual truths that had been hidden since the earth began.

To introduce this ideal regarding the mysteries, Christ said,

> Go ye into the world, saying unto all, Repent, for the kingdom of heaven has come nigh unto you. (Matthew 7:9 JST)

This command is not only a reminder of the Apostles' responsibility to take the gospel message to the world but is extended to include the membership of the Palestinian Church. The membership of the Church is to participate in calling the world to repentance. The Savior wants all men to bring their lives into harmony with the laws and commandments of the gospel. But as the gospel is taken to the world, there is a caution:

> And the mysteries of the kingdom ye shall keep within yourselves; for it is not meet to give that which is holy unto the dogs; neither cast ye your pearls unto swine, lest they trample them under their feet.
>
> For the world cannot receive that which ye, yourselves, are not able to bear; wherefore ye shall not give your pearls unto them, lest they turn again and rend you. (Matthew 7:10–11 JST)

In the Americas, the people of the Church had different responsibilities. They were not to take the gospel to the world, but their instructions were to

> give not that which is holy unto the dogs, neither cast ye your pearls before swine, lest they trample them under their feet, and turn again and rend you. (3 Nephi 14:6)

The instructions given to people in both parts of the world may seem contradictory to what the Savior had said earlier. Prior to these instructions, the righteous sought and were taught the doctrines of God's kingdom, the mysteries of their day. Now, it appears the sacred truths of the gospel were to be kept within the hierarchy of the Church. This appearance is inaccurate. If an individual has made themselves worthy, the mysteries, those doctrines not taught to the public in general such as temple ordinances, will be taught through revelation and in the appropriate place.

One source of mourning for the Saints has to do with individuals not following these instructions. Rather than teaching the first principles and ordinances of the gospel, people share the sacred doctrines of the kingdom with others not of the faith or with unprepared members. There may also be the hope that others will see the beauty of these teachings and reform their lives. But the reverse is often the case. Those unfamiliar with the gospel do not have the appropriate reverence nor the background needed for understanding, and they often ridicule the more sacred doctrines of the kingdom. Thus, the direction of the Savior is to teach the basics of the gospel (the first principles and ordinances) to those who have not prepared themselves rather than the "mysteries."

There has been a pattern established for those who desire to know the mysteries of God, which has been followed by all the prophets. Isaiah was taught,

> Whom shall he teach knowledge? And whom shall he make to understand doctrine? Them that are weaned from the milk and drawn from the breasts.
>
> For precept must be upon precept, precept upon precept; line upon line, line upon line; here a little, and there a little. (Isaiah 28:9–10; see also Doctrine and Covenants 98:12)

Paul used this principle when he wrote to the Corinthians. He taught,

> I have fed you with milk, and not with meat; for hitherto ye were not able to bear it, neither yet now are ye able. (1 Corinthians 3:2)

Those not of the faith or who are weak in the faith should be taught the basic principles of the gospel. If they accept these teachings and make themselves worthy, more knowledge is provided. It will be given a little at a time, initial knowledge providing a base for more.

At the beginning of this ideal, Christ told the disciples to instruct the Church to preach repentance. In turn Paul taught the Hebrew Saints,

> Therefore not leaving the principles of the doctrine of Christ, let us go on unto perfection; not laying again the foundation of repentance from dead works, and of faith toward God.
>
> Of the doctrine of baptisms, of laying on of hands, and of resurrection of the dead, and of eternal judgment. (Hebrew 6:1–2 JST)

Before going on to perfection, a base of doctrines must be laid. An individual must have a solid testimony of repentance from sins, faith in Christ, baptism, the resurrection of the dead, and the judgment of

God. Then, an individual will start to prepare himself to receive further knowledge. This is the doctrine of Christ.

This principle has been carried into modern days. The Prophet Joseph Smith was commanded to

> preach naught but repentance, and show not these things [mysteries] unto the world until it is wisdom in me.
>
> For they cannot bear meat now, but milk they must receive; wherefore, they must not know these things, lest they perish. (Doctrine and Covenants 19: 21–22, brackets added)

The disciples, the leaders, and the members of the Church of Christ are to teach only the doctrines of Christ as the world is invited to come unto Christ. The people of the world "cannot bear all things"; they must "grow in grace and in the knowledge of the truth" (see Doctrine and Covenants 50:40). Bruce McConkie in his Mortal Messiah series wrote,

> Any gospel truth, however easy and simple, that is not understood, or that is beyond the present spiritual capacity of a given person to understand, is to him a mystery. Faith, repentance, and baptism are mysteries to the unbelieving Gentiles. But the mysteries of the kingdom, of which Jesus here speaks, are quite another thing. This phrase has a special meaning; it refers to the deep and hidden things of the gospel—to the calculus, as it were, which can only be comprehended after the student has become proficient in arithmetic, algebra, and geometry; it refers to the temple ordinances; to the gifts of the spirit; to those things which can be known only by the power of the Holy Ghost.

> The Saints are to keep the deep and mysterious doctrines to themselves and not offer to the world more than people are able to bear. Until the newborn babe in Christ is weaned, he cannot eat meat; the milk of the world must suffice. Gospel pearls in the hands of Gentile swine enable those hoofed and snouted beasts, wallowing in the filth and swill of their rebellion and disbelief, to rend the Saints with their evil fangs. (*The Mortal Messiah* 2:161)

With these instructions, the Savior is not intending to discourage an individual from seeking after the mysteries of God once an understanding has been achieved; rather, he discourages from sharing them with the unprepared. As a young man, Nephi had "great desires to know of the mysteries of God." This desire led him to "cry unto the Lord; and behold he did visit me" (see 1 Nephi 2:16). Because of this experience, Nephi taught,

> He that diligently seeketh shall find; and the mysteries of God shall be unfolded unto them, by the power of the Holy Ghost, as well in these times as in times of old, and as well in times of old as in times to come; wherefore, the course of the Lord is one eternal round. (1 Nephi 10:19)

God is not a respecter of persons. He revealed mysteries to those who were worthy and prepared "in times of old" and will do so now and in the future. Any who diligently seek shall have the mysteries of God unfolded to them. Through the Prophet Joseph Smith, the Lord taught that diligently seeking includes keeping the commandments, working to bring forth and to establish Christ's Church, as well as not seeking for riches (see Doctrine and Covenants 6:6–7; see also Doctrine and Covenants

8:11; 11:17; Alma 26:22). Implied in all of these instructions is that the individual seeking knowledge has a deep and abiding faith in the Savior.

Any individual who follows this process will prepare themselves to receive the mysteries of God through revelation by the power of the Holy Ghost. It is under the direction of the Melchizedek Priesthood that these revelations come because this priesthood holds the key of the mysteries of the kingdom (see Doctrine and Covenants 84:19).

In his instructions, the Savior wanted his disciples to teach the people of the Church not to share the sacred doctrines, the mysteries of God, with those who have not prepared themselves. This kind of knowledge is provided a little at one time then another, line upon line, precept upon precept (see Isaiah 28:10). For

> it is given unto many to know the mysteries of God; nevertheless they are laid under a strict command that they shall not impart only according to the portion of his word which he doth grant unto the children of men, according to the heed and diligence which they give unto him. (Alma 12:9)

Summary

The ideals for this beatitude are not solely directed at the leaders of Christ's Church. Rather, these teachings are for the Apostles to teach to the general population of the Church. By following these ideals, the Saints remove some of the most common sources of sorrow and thus are comforted.

The last ideal taught by the Savior involves keeping the doctrines of the kingdom sacred. These doctrines are available to all who would keep the commandments and seek to establish the kingdom of Christ. But the mysteries will not be revealed all at once. There is a process, which begins with the basics of the first principles and ordinances of the Gospel (see Article of Faith 4) and adds upon that foundation little by little; each piece of knowledge adds to the base of testimony and prepares the recipient for the next. These sacred doctrines are not to be shared with those outside the kingdom. Those who are not prepared will belittle these sacred truths as swine trampling pearls and sorrow results.

Once again, Christ warned his disciples about hypocrisy. One area of concern amongst the Saints is when an individual who is guilty of a great sin seeks to correct another person who has a small fault. Because of their grievous sin, the individual has lost the direction of the Holy Ghost and cannot see clearly the way that should be taken. The Savior teaches that a true disciple of his examines himself or herself first and seeks to purge sin from their lives before attempting to correct others. This process allows the individual to seek for their own progress through the lens of the Holy Ghost and, as they do so, receive further clarity of vision. The Prophet Joseph Smith taught that as man becomes more like God "the clearer are his views, and the greater his enjoyments" (TPJS p. 51)

The first ideal for this beatitude involves making judgments. Each day an individual is called upon to make decisions regarding people. In this portion of the Sermon on the Mount, the Savior is instructing the Apostles to teach people to judge righteously and not condemn others. Those who use the Holy Ghost in judgment, to seek good rather than ill, will make a wise decision. There will be no cause for sorrow in either party. Another factor to be considered in passing judgment is that each person will be held to the same standard they hold others to.

If the Saints are obedient to these ideals, they will be comforted. But there is more to this beatitude than the individual ideals. By completing the Atonement, Christ provided comfort for the major sources of sorrow. In Gethsemane, he atoned for the sins of his brothers and sisters if they repented. While the redemption from sins is conditional, the Resurrection is not. It universally applies to all regardless of race, rank, or stature. Thus, the sting of the grave has been removed and comfort provided. The prophet Isaiah told Israel that "the Lord God will wipe away tears from off all faces" (see Isaiah 25:8). Christ will offer the "oil of joy for mourning, the garment of praise for the spirit of heaviness" (see Isaiah 61:3).

BLESSED ARE THE POOR IN SPIRIT

Blessed are the poor in spirit: for theirs is the Kingdom of heaven.
(Matthew 5:3)

This beatitude is not announcing that the kingdom of heaven will be populated by the depressed or humiliated. Rather, being "poor in spirit" describes those who are "humble and contrite, who have a broken heart and a contrite spirit, who are devoid of pride, self-righteousness, and self-conceit" (DNTC p. 215).

As mentioned in an earlier beatitude, one of the preeminent principles in God's plan for the exaltation of God's children is the law of moral agency. Each person in mortality is free to choose to serve God, to place his or her will subservient to that of God and to become like God or to choose the opposite (see 2 Nephi 2:27). Those who are humble or "poor in spirit" are accepting and obedient to One whose knowledge is greater than theirs. Thus, they choose to be like God. Those who are not poor in spirit bow to none.

This beatitude as given in Palestine and quoted above implies that any who is poor in spirit will comply with the ordinances and commandments of the gospel of Christ. In the Americas, Christ made sure his teachings were clear, so that there would be no misunderstanding. He taught those in Bountiful, "Blessed are the poor in spirit who come unto me" (3 Nephi 12:3). In essence, the Lord is saying, "Blessed are the poor in spirit; those who come with broken heart and a contrite spirit, believe my servants, repent of their sins, accept the ordinances of the gospel, live the commandments and endure to the end. These are they who receive the Kingdom of heaven" (refer to Doctrine and Covenants 76:50–53).

On another occasion, the Savior taught his disciples a parable about being faithful and enduring to the end (see Luke 12:35–40). Then Peter asked if the parable and the blessings for obedience were meant for the Apostles only or were available to all.

> And the Lord said, Who then is that faithful and wise steward, whom his lord shall make ruler over his household, to give them their portion of meat in due season?
>
> Blessed is that servant, whom his lord when he cometh shall find so doing.
>
> Of a truth I say unto you, that he will make him a ruler over all that he hath. (Luke 12:42–44)

The poor in spirit, all who come unto Christ and are found doing Christ's will—"theirs is the Kingdom of Heaven." They, like Christ, will be made rulers over all that God has. In his epistle to the twelve tribes of Israel, James taught this when he wrote,

> Hearken, my beloved brethren, Hath not God chosen the poor of this world rich in faith, and heirs of the Kingdom which he hath promised to them that love him? (James 2:5)

The poor of the world who are rich in faith are heirs of the kingdom. Paul wrote to the Romans,

> "For as many as are led by the Spirit of God, they are the sons of God.
>
> For ye have not received the spirit of bondage again to fear; but ye have received the spirit of adoption, whereby we cry, Abba, Father.
>
> The Spirit itself beareth witness with our spirit, that we are the children of God.
>
> And if children, then heirs; heirs of God, and joint-heirs with Christ; if so be that we suffer with him, that we may be also glorified together. (Romans 8:14–17)

The Galatians were told,

> There is neither Jew nor Greek, there is neither bond nor free, there is neither male nor female: for ye are all one in Christ Jesus.
>
> And if ye be Christ's, then are ye Abraham's seed, and heirs according to the promise. . . .
>
> Now I say, That the heir, as long as he is a child, differeth nothing from a servant, though he be lord of all;
>
> But is under tutors and governors until the time appointed of the father. . . .
>
> Wherefore thou are no more a servant, but a son; and if a son, then an heir of God through Christ. (Galatians 3:28–29; 4:1–2, 7)

John the Beloved in Revelations was told,

> To him that overcometh will I grant to sit with me in my throne, even as I also overcame, and am set down with my Father in his throne. (Revelations 3:21)

The promised blessing for the poor in spirit who come unto Christ is to be like Christ in knowledge, in dominion, in power—nothing lacking. They shall, in truth, be joint heirs with Christ. These are

> they who are the church of the Firstborn.
>
> They are they into whose hands the Fathers has given all things—
>
> They are they who are priests and kings, who have received of his fulness, and of his glory;
>
> And are priests of the Most High, after the order of Melchizedek, which was after the Order of Enoch, which was after the order of the Only Begotten Son. . . .
>
> Wherefore, all things are theirs, whether life or death, or things present, or things to come, all are theirs and they are Christ's, and Christ is Gods.
>
> And they shall over come all things. . . .
>
> These shall dwell in the presence of God and his Christ forever and ever. (Doctrine and Covenants 76:54–57, 59–60, 62)

The ideals that Christ wanted the membership of his Church taught relating to this beatitude are designed to help a person be humble before God and to come unto Christ. They will help a person become poor in spirit. In the beatitude regarding those who hunger and thirst after righteousness, the leaders in Christ's kingdom were taught about prayer and how to pray. Now those leaders are to teach members of the Church the importance of prayer. Other items Church members are to be taught include the application of the Golden Rule, entering the kingdom of heaven through the gate of ordinances, avoiding false prophets, and combining faith with works in the proper mix. Those who follow these teachings and hold out faithful to the end will receive the kingdom of God, the celestial kingdom, as their promised blessing.

Prayer

A common excuse given by people for not praying is God's omniscience. They comment, "If God knows all, he knows what I need and will give it. Why ask?" This highlights the individual's questioning of God's existence, knowledge, and power while disregarding the agency that man has. In honoring man's agency, God waits for the petition to be made. When an individual chooses not to ask, God honors that person's agency and does not answer. Because the person who makes that statement and asks that question is already doubtful when God doesn't answer the question or the condition persists, the individual assumes it "proves" that God is not omniscient, that he does not have the power to answer, or hat he does not have the knowledge needed to answer. They might even assume there is no God.

Lucifer has no desire for a person to have lines of communications to and develop a relationship with the Father of All. He prompts and tempts those he would deceive to avoid prayer. Nephi taught,

> For if ye would hearken unto the Spirit which teacheth a man to pray ye would know that ye must pray; for the evil spirit teacheth not a man to pray, but teacheth him that he must not pray. (2 Nephi 32:8)

Earlier in the Sermon on the Mount, Christ taught his Apostles how to pray. Now, he wants the Church as a body to be encouraged and instructed about prayer. The Savior told leaders of his Church on two continents,

> Say unto them, Ask of God; ask, and it shall be given unto you; seek, and ye shall find; knock, and it shall be opened unto you.
>
> For everyone that asketh, receiveth; and he that seeketh, findeth; and unto him that knocketh, it shall be opened. (Matthew 7:12–13 JST; see also 3 Nephi 13:7–8)

In these instructions, Christ outlines three levels of activity or intensity in prayer. These levels are to ask, to seek and to knock. Each step not only provides answers but helps the person develop Godlike attributes. Gerald N. Lund in his book *Hearing the Voice of the Lord* indicated there is almost an ascending order in these commands. *Asking* is a verbal action. *Seeking* is more involved where we begin to do something that uses the mind and the heart. *Knocking* is a physical action and implies that once the door is open, we will move through it.

An excellent example of asking comes from the brother of Jared. When the language was being confounded at the Tower of Babel, the brother of Jared asked the Lord not to confound his tongue or that of his family. That request was granted (see Ether 1:33–37). Then, he asked if he and his family could receive a land where they could live in peace. That request too would be granted, but they had to get there to receive it (see Ether 1:38–43). As he was constructing barges in preparation of crossing the ocean, the brother of Jared noted that there was no way to breathe since they were to travel inside an airtight vessel. When he went before the Lord in prayer, the Lord gave him the solution (see Ether 2:17–20).

Not all prayers will be answered as dramatically as a voice from heaven. The answer may come through a vision, dream, or personal visitation. It may come as a feeling or inspiration. It may come through the assistance of others. The answer may even be "no" or "not now" or something other than we expect. But prayers will be answered.

Christ taught "seek, and ye shall find" as the second level of prayer. Often, the problems people experience or the questions they have are not new. Human experience is that difficulties and questions are repeated throughout generations. As an aid to his children, God has given and continues to give revelations to his prophets and those instructions were and are recorded. In many cases, answers to questions or solutions to problems that people have can be found in the scriptures or have been addressed by prophets. If the issue has already been addressed, it isn't necessary to readdress the answer. The person is required to look it up.

During a time of religious revival, a young man, Joseph Smith, wondered which church to join. He didn't want to join just any denomination for the sake of joining; he wanted to associate with the Church of Christ. Meetings were attended and teachings compared. Because of the conflicting doctrines, young Joseph sought for answers in the Bible. While reading in James, he found a passage that instructed him to ask God as the final judge in the matter. When he did so, his prayer of faith was answered by a personal visitation from God the Father and his Son, Jesus Christ (see Joseph Smith–History 1:7–20).

As one prayerfully searches the writings of the prophets, modern and ancient, the Spirit will assist in finding the answer. Thus, "seek, and ye shall find."

Each step in the levels of prayer increases the involvement or effort required of the individual. The first level is to exercise faith in Christ and ask in simple prayer. Next combines the first with seeking for answers among the words of God's prophets. The last level—knocking—is the most involved. One must study the issue, weigh the alternatives, gauge the consequences of those alternatives, and come to a conclusion. At that point, the individual goes before God for a confirmation or rejection of that decision. Christ told Oliver Cowdery that

> you must study it out in your mind; then you must ask me if it be right, and if it is right I will cause that your bosom shall burn within you; therefore, you shall feel that it is right.
>
> But if it be not right you shall have no such feelings, but you shall have a stupor of thought that shall cause you to forget the thing which is wrong. (Doctrine and Covenants 9:8–9)

This process of researching the issues and evaluating the options helps further the development of the individual. It goes beyond simply answering the question or solving a problem. It helps that person develop analytical skills and become more like God.

An example of this level of prayer can also be taken from the brother of Jared. After the barges referred to earlier had been completed and the issue of fresh air resolved, another problem was noted: there was no light in the vessels. The brother of Jared went to the Lord in prayer, expecting a solution to be given as before. Instead of solving the problem, the Lord asked the brother of Jared to develop his own solution and then gave reasons against windows (see Ether 2:22–25). In response to this challenge, the brother of Jared went into the mountains, made sixteen glass balls, asked the Lord to touch the balls, and have them provide light for the barges (see Ether 3:1–5). This solution not only provided the needed illumination in the ships but allowed the brother of Jared to see the spirit form of the Savior (see Ether 3:6–16).

Besides the manner of prayer and the levels of involvement, there are principles which must be followed for prayers to be answered or the answers to be recognized. These principles help prepare the individual to be receptive and able to hear and accept the answer. In effect, by using these principles, the person becomes poor in spirit.

All the following principles, of course, assume the first: faith in God the Father, his Son, Jesus Christ, and in the Holy Ghost. The Prophet Joseph Smith taught as "faith is the moving cause of all action in temporal concerns, so it is in spiritual" (refer to *Lectures on Faith* 1:12, p. 8). If the supplicant does not have faith in the Godhead, he or she will not pray or expect answers.

Another principle of prayer is that of rendering obedience to God's commandments. Bruce R. McConkie wrote in *Mormon Doctrine* that

> obedience is the first law of heaven, the cornerstone upon which all righteousness and progression rest. It consists in compliance with divine law, in conformity to the mind and will of Deity, in complete subjection to God and his commandments. To obey gospel law is to yield obedience to the Lord, to execute the commands of and be ruled by him whose we are. (*Mormon Doctrine*, p. 539)

In a general epistle to the Church, the Apostle John taught,

> And whatsoever we ask, we receive of him, because we keep his commandments, and do those things that are pleasing in his sight. (1 John 3:22)

When a person shows their humility by choosing to do those things that are pleasing in God's sight, they receive the promised blessing. They can be confident of receiving or recognizing answers to prayers. Those who are disobedient will not have God's spirit and resist God's answer nor will they confess his hand in all things.

Nephi, who left Jerusalem with his father, adds a principle in addition to that of faith and obedience. He taught his rebellious older brothers,

> Do ye not remember the things which the Lord hath said?—
> If you will not harden your hearts, and ask me in faith, believing that ye shall receive, with diligence in keeping my commandments, surely these things shall be made known unto you. (1 Nephi 15:11)

Those who approach the Lord are to do so without "hard hearts." They are not to resist the answer even if it conflicts with any preexisting ideas they might have. Nephi also taught that the supplicant is to expect an answer while obeying the commandments.

Another principle of prayer is to ask for what is appropriate. Nephi later wrote,

> Yea, I know that God will give liberally to him that asketh. Yea, my God will give me, if I ask not amiss. (2 Nephi 4:35)

In more modern times, the Lord told the Prophet Joseph Smith,

> Draw near unto me and I will draw near unto you; seek me diligently and ye shall find me; ask, and ye shall receive; knock, and it shall be opened unto you.
>
> Whatsoever ye ask the Father in my name it shall be given unto you, that is expedient for you;
>
> And if ye ask anything that is not expedient for you, it shall turn to your condemnation. (Doctrine and Covenants 88:63–65)

God will grant answers to those who ask not amiss or ask for that which is expedient. President Joseph Fielding Smith taught,

> In our praying we should seek to do the will of the Lord and not merely to reap some advantage or gratification

which may not be the best for us. This is a very significant saying [Sec 88:63–65 quoted]. Therefore we should not be too insistent, but should pray earnestly seeking light and to know the will of the Lord, with an unselfish spirit. Then, with this spirit, will our bodies be filled with light. (*Latter-day Prophets and the Doctrine & Covenants* 3:177)

After Christ told his disciples to teach the people of his church about prayer the Apostles in Palestine raised a concern.

> And then said his disciples unto him, they will say unto us, We ourselves are righteous, and need not that any man should teach us. God, we know, heard Moses and some of the prophets; but us he will not hear.
>
> And they will say, We have the law for our salvation, and that is sufficient for us. (Matthew 7:14–15 JST)

The Apostles are not trying to be obstructive. Their occupations were geared toward survival and trade, and they were not trained to teach or debate. In raising these items, their desire was to anticipate any objections they might face and wondered how those objections should be answered. First, the Apostles pointed out that those being taught would claim to be righteous, and because of their righteousness, they didn't need anyone to teach them. There was the added obstacle that the Apostles hadn't attended one of the recognized rabbinical schools and wouldn't be recognized as teachers of the people.

A second objection mentioned is directly related to prayer. The Apostles worried that people would say that God listened to prophets' entreaties centuries earlier and replied. That was then, but God does not answer now. But since Moses established God's laws of performances, it would be sufficient for salvation.

Both objections that had the Apostles concerned deny modern revelation and the Father's willingness to answer prayers.

> Then Jesus answered, and said unto his disciples, thus shall ye say unto them.
>
> What man among you, having a son, and he shall be standing out, and shall say, Father, open thy house that I may come in and sup with thee, and will not say, Come in, my son; for mine is thine, and thine is mine? . . .
>
> Or what man is there of you, whom if his son ask bread, will give him a stone?
>
> Or if he ask a fish, will he give him a serpent?
>
> If ye then, being evil, know how to give good gifts unto your children, how much more shall your Father which is in heaven give good things to them that ask him? (Matthew 7:16–17 JST; Matthew 7:9–11; see also 3 Nephi 13:9–11)

How does the Savior instruct his Apostles to answer these objections?

> That their supplications would be heard and answered followed as a rich promise. They were to ask and they would receive; they were to knock and the door would be opened. Surely the Heavenly Father would not be less considerate than a human parent; and what father would answer his son's plea for bread by giving him a stone, or who would give a serpent when a fish was desired? With greater certainty would God bestow good gifts upon those who asked according to their need, in faith. (*Jesus the Christ*, p. 245)

God has promised answers to prayers, and he does not lie. Yes, he answered the prayers of Moses and Isaiah. They received answers because they made themselves worthy and were ready to be obedient to God's will. Our Heavenly Father will answer the prayers and supplications of those who comply with his wishes (see Doctrine and Covenants 82:10; 130:20–21). But answers will be given at a time and in a manner of His choosing.

The Golden Rule

Over the years, a joke has been made about the Golden Rule. It is said that "he who has the gold makes the rules." The philosophy shown in that joke is the antithesis of what Christ wanted his Saints to be. Included in this beatitude is a more compassionate Golden Rule which the Savior wanted the Saints to be taught:

> Therefore all things whatsoever ye would that men should do to you, do ye even so to them: for this is the law and the prophets. (Matthew 7:12; see also 3 Nephi 13:12)

Regarding this commandment, President Joseph F. Smith said,

> We need mercy; then let us be merciful. We need charity; let us be charitable. We need forgiveness; let us forgive. Let us do unto others what we would that they should do unto us. (*Gospel Doctrine*, p. 339)

The principle of righteous living embodied in the Golden Rule seems simple, yet it encapsulates the teachings of all the prophets regarding relationships with other people. If the members of Christ's Church followed this rule, they would be exemplars of the other Beatitudes. As President Smith indicated, they would be merciful because they desired to receive mercy. They would love others because they desired to be loved. They would be charitable and forgiving, seeking righteous judgment, because they desired to be treated likewise.

President Gordon B. Hinckley spoke of the importance of living the Golden Rule. He wrote,

> I desire to touch on one of the most commonly known and probably the least observed of the Lord's commandments – that which has come to be known as the Golden Rule.
>
> Said Jesus: "Whatsoever ye would that men should do to you, do ye even so to them." (Matthew 7:12)
>
> May I remind us at this Christmas season that if only each of us would reflect occasionally on that Christ-given mandate and make an effort to observe it, this would be a different world. There would be greater happiness in our homes; there would be kinder feelings among our associates; there would be much less of litigation and a greater effort to compose differences. There would be a new measure of love and appreciation and respect.
>
> There would be more generous hearts, more thoughtful consideration and concern, and a greater desire to spread the gospel of peace and to advance the work of salvation among the children of men. (*Ensign*, December 1991)

He adds an example from the life of Spencer W. Kimball:

> I would like to tell you of another who lived the Golden Rule. Many already know part of the story. It occurred a few years ago in the winter at O'Hare International Airport, that great and busy place that serves the city of Chicago. On this occasion a severe storm had caused delays and cancellations of flights. The thousands of people stranded or delayed there were impatient and cross and

irritable. Among those in trouble was a woman, a young mother standing in a long line at the check-in counter. She had a two-year-old child who was on the dirty floor at her feet. She was pregnant with another child. She was sick and weary to the bone. Her doctor had warned her against bending and picking up anything heavy, so as she moved slowly with the line she pushed her crying and hungry child with her foot. People who saw her made critical and cutting remarks, but none offered to help.

Then a man came toward her and with a smile of kindness on his face said, "You need help. Let me help you." He lifted the dirty, crying child from the floor and held her warmly in his arms. Taking a stick of gum from his pocket, he gave it to the child. Its sweet taste calmed her. He explained to those in the line the woman's need of help, then took her to the head of the line, spoke with the ticket agent, and soon had her checked in. He then found seats where she and her child could be comfortable, chatted for a moment, and disappeared into the crowd without giving his name. She went on her way to her home in Michigan.

Years later there came to the office of the President of the Church a letter which reads as follows:

"Dear President Kimball:

I am a student at Brigham Young University. I have just returned from my mission in Munich, West Germany. I had a lovely mission and learned much. . . .

I was sitting in priesthood meeting last week, when a story was told of a loving service which you performed some twenty-one years ago in the Chicago airport. The story told of how you met a young pregnant mother with a . . . screaming child, in . . . distress, waiting in a long line for her tickets. She was threatening miscarriage and therefore couldn't lift her child to comfort her. She had experienced four previous miscarriages, which gave added reason for the doctors orders not to bend or lift.

You comforted the crying child and explained the dilemma to the other passengers in line. This act of love took the strain and tension off my mother. I was born a few months later in Flint, Michigan.

I just want to thank you for your love. Thank you for your example." (*Ensign*, December 1991)

Entrance to the Kingdom

Enter ye in at the strait gate: for wide is the gate, and broad is the way, that leadeth to destruction, and many there be which go in thereat:

Because strait is the gate, and narrow is the way, which leadeth unto life, and few there be that find it. (Matthew 7:13–14; see also 3 Nephi 14:13–14)

The leaders of Christ's Church are to teach those who desire to follow the Savior and enter his kingdom must do so in the manner outlined by the Savior. There can be no substitution of manner or process. This is in accordance with the Apostles' charge from the Savior to maintain the ordinances and doctrines of the kingdom in their purity. The gate by which people enter the kingdom is "strait," meaning restricted, constricted, narrow, tight, strict, or exacting (see *Websters New World Dictionary*, Third Edition, p. 1323).

The strait gate mentioned by the Savior is baptism and receipt of the gift of the Holy Ghost. At the very beginning of his mortal ministry in Palestine, the Savior sought out baptism (see Matthew 3:13–17), which provided the example for all of God's children to follow. After seeing this ordinance performed in vision, Nephi taught his people,

> Wherefore, do the things which I have told you I have seen that your Lord and your Redeemer should do; for, for this cause have they been shown unto me, that ye might know the gate by which ye should enter. For the gate by which ye should enter is repentance and baptism by water; and then cometh a remission of your sins by fire and by the Holy Ghost. (2 Nephi 32:17)

In order for an individual to follow Christ and enter God's kingdom, he or she must repent of their sins and receive the entrance ordinances of baptism and the gift of the Holy Ghost. Compliance with these ordinances will provide the individual with a remission of sins, which is necessary for one to enter the celestial kingdom "for no unclean thing can dwell with God" (see 1 Nephi 10:21).

Not all baptisms performed in the world will have the effect desired. To be accepted of God, these ordinances must be performed in the strict or exacting manner outlined by the Savior and his prophets by one holding the proper priesthood authority (see Doctrine and Covenants 20:72–74).

The adversary would have the world believe that there are many ways to return to God and that there is a wide gate of types of baptism. Some denominations teach baptism is not required to be with our Father but is offered if desired. Because the baptisms of those denominations who offer the ordinance are not sanctioned of God and are not performed in the manner specified or with the priesthood of God, they are not effective.

In addition to differing methods and needs for ordinances, the way is broad with many different teachings. The Savior taught the way back to God is narrow, with specific doctrines and commandments that lead to exaltation. Care must be taken to listen for the confirming Spirit which attends gospel truth. Alienation from God—spiritual death—is the result for those who do not enter the gate or walk on the path as specified by the Savior.

Entrance to the kingdom of heaven through the strait gate is not a multiple answer question. Even Christ, one who was perfect and had no sin, complied with the necessary requirements. The prophet Nephi discussed the baptism of the Savior by saying,

> And now, if the Lamb of God, he being holy, should have need to be baptized by water, to fulfill all righteousness, O then, how much more need have we, being unholy, to be baptized, yea, even by water!
>
> And now, I would ask of you, my beloved brethren, wherein the Lamb of God did fulfill all righteousness in being baptized by water?
>
> Know ye not that he was holy? But notwithstanding he being holy, he showeth unto the children of men that, according to the flesh he humbleth himself before the Father, and witnesseth unto the Father that he would be obedient unto him in keeping his commandments.
>
> Wherefore, after he was baptized with water the Holy Ghost descended upon him in the form of a dove.
>
> And again, it showeth unto the children of men the straitness of the path, and the narrowness of the gate, by

which they should enter, he having set the example before them. (2 Nephi 31:5–9)

McConkie in his Mortal Messiah series writes,

> Enter in at the strait gate of baptism; find yourself on the strait and narrow path leading to the celestial kingdom. Enter in at the strait gate of celestial marriage; find yourself on the strait and narrow path leading to eternal life in the highest heaven of the celestial world. The broad gate is always open, and all the influences of the world urge and entice men to enter and go downward to darkness; the narrow gate is open only to those who desire righteousness and who seek the Lord and his goodness. (*The Mortal Messiah* 2:167)

God is not the author of confusion (see 1 Corinthians 14:33). His requirements for entry into his kingdom are exacting. There are not many ideas of Christ—just one. There are not many baptisms—just one (see Ephesians 4:5). There are no conflicting doctrines in his kingdom.

In a prior beatitude, the Savior charged the leaders of his Church to keep the doctrines and ordinances of the gospel pure. Here, the Saints are to receive a companion charge. They must receive the ordinances sanctioned by God and hold to the doctrines that are exalting. Those who are obedient and receive the necessary ordinances at the hands of the priesthood enter the gate and begin to walk the path that leads to eternal life. Christ was the exemplar. Although he was holy, he was baptized to show his obedience and to designate the path for those who followed.

False Prophets

Through the ages, God has taught and directed his people through men called prophets. These righteous men selected by God teach of his character, showing how he has dealt with mankind in the past. The prophet also has the responsibility to denounce sin, foretell its punishment, and redress wrongs (see "Prophet" in *Bible Dictionary*, p. 754). God directing his work through mortal servants is called the law of prophets. The only time a prophet will not be present among God's children is when those children are wicked and reject those sent by God. As God and Christ do not change but are "the same yesterday, and today, and forever" (see Hebrews 13:8), God will continue to reveal his will to men through prophets. Many years before Christ's ministry, the children of Israel were told that "God will do nothing, until he revealeth his secret unto his servants the prophets" (Amos 3:7 JST). After the Savior's ascension into heaven, the Apostles directed the Church organized by Christ. During that time, the Apostle Paul wrote to the Ephesians that the Church of Christ is "built upon the foundation of apostles and prophets" (see Ephesians 2:20).

After the instruction that the Apostles are to teach their fellow Saints about the gate by which they should enter and the path they should follow to receive the kingdom of heaven, a warning is issued:

> Beware of false prophets, which come to you in sheep's clothing, but inwardly they are ravening wolves. (Matthew 7:15; see also 3 Nephi 14:15)

Lucifer is well aware that God works through prophets to aid in the exaltation of God's children. To thwart God's efforts, the adversary sends his counterfeits. Thus, Church leaders are to warn the Church about following false prophets. The Church is cautioned that these men and women, Lucifer's counterfeits, would appear as true prophets seeking only to help their brothers and sisters at God's request, but they are actually seeking wealth or power. Bruce R. McConkie in the second volume of his Mortal Messiah series contrasted a true prophet from one who is false. He wrote that

> a true prophet is one who has the testimony of Jesus; one who knows by personal revelation that Jesus Christ is the Son of the Living God, and that he was to be—or has been—crucified for the sins of the world; one to whom God speaks and who recognized the still small voice of the Spirit. A true prophet is one who holds the holy priesthood; who is a legal administrator; who has power and authority from God to represent him on earth. A true prophet is a teacher of righteousness to whom the truths of the gospel have been revealed and who present them to his fellowmen so they can become heirs of salvation in the highest heaven. A true prophet is a witness, a living witness, one who knows, and one who testifies. Such a one, if need be, foretells the future and reveals to men what the Lord reveals to him.
>
> A false prophet is the opposite of all this. He does not know by personal revelation of the divine Sonship of the Prophet who was like unto Moses. He does not enjoy the gift of the Holy Ghost or hold the holy priesthood; and he is not a legal administrator who has power to bind and seal on earth and in heaven. He is not a teacher of true doctrine; he may believe any of an infinite variety of false doctrines, but he does not teach, in purity and perfection, the fulness of the everlasting gospel. Because he does not receive revelation or enjoy the gifts of the Spirit, he believes these things have ceased. He thinks "God, I know, heard Moses and some of the prophets; but me he will not hear." Because he teaches

false doctrines, he does not lead men to salvation, and in cases not a few he becomes a ravening wolf in sheep's clothing. (*The Mortal Messiah* 2:169–170)

The Saints were warned to be on the watch for false prophets and avoid them for the consequences of following a false prophet are disastrous. In the July 1976 *Ensign*, Neil J. Flinders told of an experience he had as a young man in northern Utah which reinforced the importance of knowing who to follow:

> When I was a boy, I used to go with my father to the Ogden stockyards. We lived on a small farm and occasionally sold a few animals there. During one of these visits my father taught me a lesson that has increased in its value over the years. It was a spontaneous bit of instruction and probably took less than a minute to deliver.
>
> The holding pens for the cattle, hogs and sheep were on the river bank. A fenced bridge spanned the river and connected with a ramp that angled up to the top story of a processing plant on the other bank. Since the animals to be butchered had to be herded across the bridge and up the ramp, the men who managed this operation developed a clever solution. They trained a black goat to enter the sheep pens, mingle with the sheep and then lead the way across the bridge and up the ramp through the door of the processing plant. Once inside the doorway, the goat stepped aside, and the sheep pressed on to their ultimate fate.
>
> I remember watching this scene as my dad explained the operation. He paused, then added, "Let that be a lesson to

you; be careful who you follow. Make sure you know where you are being led." (Neil J. Flinders, *Ensign*, p.)

This example, like the Savior's warning, is pointed. A fake prophet does not have the authority to perform ordinances nor does he or she teach the doctrines of exaltation. A person following a false prophet will not be exalted.

After warning Church members to be careful of whom they follow, the Apostles in Palestine and disciples in the Americas were to teach the Saints how to discern between a false or true prophet. Christ said,

> Ye shall know them by their fruits. Do men gather grapes of thorns, or figs of thistles? Even so every good tree bringeth forth good fruit; but a corrupt tree bringeth forth evil fruit.
>
> A good tree cannot bring forth evil fruit, neither can a corrupt tree bring forth good fruit. Every tree that bringeth not forth good fruit is hewn down, and cast into the fire. Wherefore by their fruits ye shall know them. (Matthew 7:16–20; see also 3 Nephi 14:16–20)

How are the Saints to recognize a true prophet of God?

> "Ye shall know them by their fruits," Jesus said. By their fruits—their words, their acts, the wonders that they do—these things shall separate true prophets and teachers from false ones. Do they receive revelations and see visions? Does the Holy Ghost speak by their mouth? Are they legal administers who have power to bind and seal on earth and in heaven? Is their doctrine true and sound and in harmony with all that is found in Holy Writ? Do they enjoy the gifts of the Spirit, so that the sick are healed under their hands? And

does the Lord God give his Holy Spirit to attest the truth of their words and to approve the acts that they do? Without true prophets there is no salvation; false prophets lead people astray; men choose, at the peril of their salvation, the prophets whom they follow. (*The Mortal Messiah* 2:170–171)

Faith & Works

The Savior closes this beatitude by instructing the leaders of His Church to teach the membership of the Church about the relationship of faith and works. Christ said,

> Not every one that saith unto me, Lord, Lord shall enter into the Kingdom of heaven; but he that doeth the will of my Father which is in heaven. For the day soon cometh, that men shall come before me to judgment, to be judged according to their works. (Matthew 7:21 JST; see also 3 Nephi 14:21)

Members of Christ's Church must have more than faith or expressions of faith to enter God's kingdom. Faith must be coupled with obedience to God's will to achieve the desired result. Each person must receive the necessary ordinances and press forward, studying the scriptures and enduring whatever is asked until the end. Those who do so receive eternal life (see 2 Nephi 31:19–20). Thus, Christ taught that "not everyone that saith unto me, Lord, Lord shall enter into the Kingdom of Heaven; but he that doeth the will of my Father."

Bruce R. McConkie wrote,

> Lip service alone does not save; it is not confessing that Jesus is the Lord, without more, that opens heaven's door; belief

without works has no saving power. Keep the commandments; do the will of the Father; work and labor and struggle and strive—then expect salvation." (*The Mortal Messiah* 2:172)

James addressed this issue in an epistle to the scattered tribes of Israel. He wrote,

> What profit is it, my brethren, for a man to say he hath faith, and hath not works? Can faith save him?
>
> Yea, a man may say, I will show thee I have faith without works: but I say, show me thy faith without works, and I will show thee my faith by my works.
>
> For if a brother or sister be naked and destitute, and one of you say, Depart in peace, be warmed and filled: notwithstanding he give not those things which are needful to the body: what profit is your faith unto such?
>
> Even so faith, if it hath not works is dead, being alone.
>
> Therefore wilt thou know, o vain man, that faith without works is dead and cannot save you?
>
> Thou believest there is one God; thou doest well; the devils also believe, and tremble; thou hast made themselves like unto them, not being justified.
>
> Was not Abraham our father justified by works, when he had offered Isaac his son upon the altar?
>
> Seest thou how works are wrought with his faith, and by works was faith made perfect?
>
> And the scripture was fulfilled which saith, Abraham believeth God, and it was imputed unto him for righteousness: and he was called the Friend of God.

> Ye see then how that by works a man is justified, and not by faith only.
>
> Likewise also was not Rahab the harlot justified by works, when she had received the messengers, and had sent them out another way?
>
> For as the body without the spirit is dead, so faith without works is dead also. (James 2:14-26 JST)

Faith in Christ is the first principle of the gospel. But faith alone cannot exalt a person. Faith and works must be combined for an individual to be saved. What works? Those done by the Savior. Enter by the gate and continue to the temple. Assist those in need and your faith will be made whole.

The last portion of these instructions regarding judgment was not passed to the Saints in the Americas. It appears that those in the New World were not as steeped in works as the Jews. After instructing the Saints about the fallacy of relying on faith alone, Christ talks about the other extreme: relying on works without faith for exaltation.

> Many will say to me in that day, Lord, Lord, have we not prophesied in thy name? And in thy name have cast out devils? And in thy name done many wonderful works?
>
> And then will I profess unto them, I never knew you: depart from me, ye that work iniquity. (Matthew 7:22-23; see also 3 Nephi 14:22-23)

At the time these instructions were given in Palestine, those who were taught the gospel of Christ came from the house of Israel, more specifically from the tribe of Judah. They had lived their entire lives with the strictness of the practices, traditions, ordinances, and sacrifices related to the law of Moses. Through the preceding centuries, the intent of the law, that of developing faith in the Messiah to come, had been forgotten. These people failed to recognize that all their sacrifices and all their works had no power to exalt without the atonement of the Messiah they were looking for. On another continent, Mosiah told his people,

> The Lord God saw that his people were a stiffnecked people, and he appointed unto them a law, even the Law of Moses.
>
> And many signs, and wonders, and types, and shadows showed he unto them, concerning his coming; and also holy prophets spake unto them concerning his coming; and yet they hardened their hearts, and understood not that the Law of Moses availeth nothing except it were through the atonement of his blood. (Mosiah 3:14–15)

Just as faith without works is dead so also is works without faith. Bruce R. McConkie wrote that the Savior's message about works refers to

> those of the elders of Israel who are true ministers; who have been on missions for the Church, for instance; who have healed the sick and performed great miracles; but who did not magnify their callings all their lives and thereby endure in righteousness to the end. (DNTC 1:255)

An individual may have performed many acts of service with the priesthood of God and may have prophesied and cast out devils but failed to endure to the end. The result is apostasy. When the judgment of those individuals is held, the Savior says, "Depart from me, ye that work iniquity."

The category of those who claim to have performed miracles or performed mighty works in the name of Christ is not limited to those who rightfully held the priesthood of God for a time. It also includes the following:

> False ministers, those who have professed to teach the gospel, but who have acted without authority from God. Included in this group are all teachers of religion—whether pagan, Jewish, Christian, or of whatever classification—who have not been 'called of God, by prophecy, and by the laying on of hands, by those who are in authority, to preach the Gospel and administer in the ordinances thereof' (Fifth Article of Faith). Some of these are ministers who have so completely sold themselves to Satan that they have worked miracles by his power. (DNTC 1:255)

Those who desire to be numbered among the Church of Christ must understand the interaction of faith and works. Both are required for the exaltation of the individual.

Those who rely on the receipt of ordinances and obedience to the commandments while neglecting faith in Christ will not be exalted. The Apostle Paul wrote to the saints of Ephesus that it is

> by grace are ye saved through faith; and that not of yourselves: it is the gift of God.
>
> Not of works, lest any man should boast. (Ephesians 2:8–9)

On another continent and a century earlier, the prophet Alma described this principle in a different manner. He said,

> And since man had fallen he could not merit anything of himself; but the sufferings and death of Christ atone for their sins, through faith and repentance, and so forth; and

that he breaketh the bands of death, that the grave shall have no victory, and that the sting of death should be swallowed up in the hopes of glory. (Alma 22:14)

In order to be worthy of the kingdom of heaven, the celestial kingdom, each person must qualify. He or she must receive the saving and exalting ordinances as specified by God while recognizing the Savior's efforts on their behalf. This recognition of Christ comes as a person is spiritually born of God by having a mighty change of heart (see Alma 5:14, 19). It is through the appropriate combination of works and faith that a person is exalted.

Summary

This beatitude completes the Sermon on the Mount and also completes the outline of what Church leaders are to teach the general membership of the Church. All these ideals direct the Saints to Christ. Broken hearts and contrite spirits are developed as each person complies with the Savior's instructions.

The last ideal the Savior taught was for an individual to use faith and works in the proper combination. At the time these teachings were given, the house of Israel was steeped in works. They had forgotten that it is by the sacrifice of Christ that the ordinances of the gospel had been and are made effective. A person may do good deeds, work miracles, and receive the exalting ordinances, but if he or she does not have faith in Christ and is not spiritually reborn, all those works are fruitless. The reverse is also true. Exaltation will not be received by those who do not comply with the specified ordinances and live as they profess. If one has true faith, he or she will comply with all the requirements of Christ—receive the ordinances and obey the commandments.

The Saints were also warned about following false prophets. Our Father in Heaven has taught his people through the ages using prophets. This pattern had been established at the beginning of man's history and continued. Care has to be exercised by the Saints in whom they follow for evil and designing men assume the appearance of righteousness as a means to achieve power, fame, or wealth. These wolves in sheeps' clothing lead those who follow them away from the celestial kingdom. The Lord provided a key in discerning a false prophet from a true prophet of God: look at their fruits. A true prophet follows the order established by God, is called by God to teach the gospel of Christ, and the Holy Ghost attends. A false prophet appoints himself or herself or is selected by popular acclaim. A false prophet teaches man's ideas combined with scriptures rather than God's saving doctrines, and the Spirit does not confirm the message given.

Entrance into the kingdom of God through ordinances was also discussed. In order to enter the celestial kingdom, each person must receive the required ordinances at the hands of one holding the proper authority. The first ordinance required, baptism and receiving the gift of the Holy Ghost, is considered the entrance ordinance that puts one on the path to exaltation. Other ordinances necessary for exaltation include receipt of the priesthood for worthy males and those found in the temple, including temple marriage. Jesus Christ, although a perfect being, insisted on complying with the requirements and received baptism at the hand of John the Baptist in order to fulfill all righteousness (see Matthew 3:15). He set the example of obedience for all to follow.

The Saints were also to be taught how they should treat each other. This teaching has come to be known as the Golden Rule. Each person is to treat others as he or she would like to be treated.

The first ideal to be taught for this beatitude was about prayer. In order to develop a broken heart and a contrite spirit, each person must be in communication with their Father in Heaven. There are three levels of this communication with the first being to simply ask. A question cannot be answered or comfort given if the request is not made. Agency requires that the request be made. For the Father to do otherwise would imperil agency.

Another level of prayer involves the individual searching through the writings of modern and ancient prophets to find their answers. The human condition is such that problems and questions are repeated throughout generations. God will answer prayers, but it is not necessary for him to re-reveal gospel principles. He will guide a prayerful individual to the answer he or she is seeking.

The last level of prayer includes the prior levels and further develops the individual. As each person seeks for an answer, they come to a resolution or decision based on their research then asks for a confirmation by the Spirit. The answer comes in the form of a confirming "burning in the bosom" or a stupor of thought if the decision is wrong. One cannot be like the Father of All if one cannot analyze problems and develop solutions like the brother of Jared.

By following the ideals of prayer, the golden rule, receiving ordinances, following true prophets, and combining faith with works, a person develops the attitude of being poor in spirit. This state is not one of depression. It is when one is humble and obedient and results in joy. The scriptures describe this as having a broken heart and a contrite spirit.

The promised blessing for achieving this state is the kingdom of heaven. The Lord told the Prophet Joseph Smith,

> If thou wilt do good, yea, and hold out faithful to the end, thou shalt be saved in the kingdom of God, which is the greatest of all the gifts of God; for there is no gift greater than the gift of salvation. (Doctrine and Covenants 6:13)

This greatest of all the gifts of God, the gift of salvation and the kingdom of God or heaven, has a modern term: the celestial kingdom. This is where God dwells (see *Mormon Doctrine*, p. 417). Those who enter this kingdom are the poor in spirit.

SUMMARY

"Therefore, whosoever heareth . . ." (Matthew 7:24)

The main portion of the Sermon on the Mount has been completed. All that remained was for the Savior to summarize all that had been taught. Rather than touch again on each item that had been discussed, he spoke of the importance of being obedient and of doing. Christ said,

> Therefore whosoever heareth these sayings of mine, and doeth them, I will liken him unto a wise man, which built his house upon a rock:
>
> And the rain descended, and the floods came, and the winds blew, and beat upon that house; and it fell not: for it was founded upon a rock.
>
> And everyone that heareth these sayings of mine, and doeth them not, shall be likened unto a foolish man, which built his house upon the sand:
>
> And the rain descended, and the floods came, and the winds blew, and it beat upon that house; and it fell: and great was the fall of it." (Matthew 7:24–27; see also 3 Nephi 14: 24–27)

Luke also recorded a version of these instructions.

> And why call ye me, Lord, Lord, and do not the things which I say?
>
> Whosoever cometh to me, and heareth my sayings, and doeth them, I will shew unto you to whom he is like:
>
> He is like a man which built an house, and digged deep, and laid the foundation on a rock: and when the flood arose, the stream beat vehemently upon that house, and could not shake it, for it was founded upon a rock.
>
> But he that heareth, and doeth not, is like a man that without a foundation built an house upon the earth; against which the stream did beat vehemently, and immediately it fell; and the ruin of that house was great. (Luke 6:46–49)

In construction, the type of soil upon which to build is of vital importance. For a house to stand, a more stable or solid foundation is required. In the parable quoted above, Christ points out that those who listen to the teachings contained in the Sermon on the Mount and put those teachings into everyday use digs deep to lay the foundation of their souls upon stone—the sure foundation of Christ and his teachings. Those who hear and do not act appropriately build upon sand or the philosophies of man, which are easily undermined. When the storms of life and floods of temptation come, as they will, those who have based their soul on that which shifts will be swept away.

King Benjamin used this imagery of rock and storm when he taught his sons to base their lives on Christ:

> And now my sons, remember, remember that it is upon the rock of our Redeemer, who is Christ, the Son of God, that ye must build your foundations; that when the devil shall send forth his mighty winds, yea, his shafts in the whirlwind, yea,

when all his hail and his mighty storm shall beat upon you; it shall have no power to drag you down to the gulf of misery and endless wo, because of the rock upon which ye are built, which is a sure foundation, a foundation whereon if men build they cannot fall. (Helaman 5:12)

Prior to delivering the Sermon on the Mount to his leaders in the Americas, the Savior also used this imagery when he said,

And again I say unto you, ye must repent, and be baptized in my name, and become as a little child, or ye can in no wise inherit the Kingdom of God.

Verily, verily, I say unto you, that this is my doctrine, and whoso buildeth upon this buildeth upon my rock, and the gates of hell shall not prevail against them.

And whoso shall declare more or less than this, and establish it for my doctrine, the same cometh of evil, and is not built upon my rock; but he buildeth upon a sandy foundation, and the gates of hell stand open to receive such when the floods come and the winds beat upon them. (3 Nephi 11:38–40)

In this latter-day dispensation, the Savior is more direct. He told the Prophet Joseph Smith,

Wherefore, I am in your midst, and I am the good shepherd, and the stone of Israel. He that buildeth upon this rock shall never fall. (Doctrine and Covenants 50:44)

The scriptures stress that if a person hears and keeps the commandments of God, if they receive the ordinances of salvation at the hands of one who holds the Priesthood of God, if they pray, are charitable, are merciful and forgiving, and follow the other teachings of Christ, that person will have a life focused or based upon Christ. The teachings of the Savior are eternal truths; they are sure. They do not shift or change with the whims or desires of men, and the blessings resulting from obedience help any person endure all the trials, temptations, and disappointments that life brings. The person who hears and obeys will stand strong against the adversary.

A person who builds his or her life upon any foundation other than Christ base their lives on foundations that shifts with the vagaries of man. Just as a house built upon sand crumbles when the river rises, so do the lives of men who are not centered on Christ. They will not have the spiritual strength to withstand the storms of Satan. This person will not be merciful or forgive when asked, will not be charitable when needed, and will not be concerned about retaining the doctrines and ordinances of exaltation in their saving purity. This person fails in their promise and falls short in the objective of returning to be with God the Father and his Son, Jesus Christ. By hearing but not obeying the Savior, this person refuses the blessings promised. He or she chooses not to enter the kingdom of heaven.

> And now it came to pass that when Jesus had ended these sayings he cast his eyes round about on the multitude, and said unto them: Behold, ye have heard the things which I taught before I ascended to my Father; therefore, whoso remembereth these sayings of mine and doeth them, him will I raise up at the last day. (3 Nephi 15:1)

In the Americas, Christ reiterated his instructions to live what he had just finished teaching and specified a blessing. This is a further reinforcement that he expects the Saints to actually live his teachings. Those who remember what he taught and obey will be raised at the last day when Christ returns crowned with glory,

There are blessings attached to each beatitude. If a leader desires to receive that blessing, he or she must obey the beatitude to which that blessing is attached (see Doctrine and Covenants 130:20–21). In other words, if the leader endures persecution while maintaining the purity of the doctrines and integrity of the ordinances and if that person is an example of living the gospel, that person will receive the kingdom of heaven. Those who are peacemakers become the children of God.

All of the blessings associated with the Beatitudes point the obedient to the celestial kingdom. The obedient receive the kingdom of heaven, become the children of God, see God, obtain mercy, are filled with the Holy Ghost, inherit the earth, and receive comfort.

Many have expressed the desire to receive these blessings and return to God but have not listened to and obeyed the teachings of Christ or received the necessary ordinances. Thus, leaders of the Church are to teach that "not every one that saith unto [Christ], Lord, Lord, shall enter into the Kingdom of heaven; but he that doeth the will of my Father which is in heaven" (see Matthew 7:21 JST). Entrance into God's kingdom is gained only upon the terms set by God the Father. There is no other way.

Later in his Palestinian ministry, the Savior taught this principle to his disciples in a parable.

> The Kingdom of heaven is like unto a certain King, which made a marriage for his son,
> And sent forth his servants to call them that were bidden to the wedding: and they would not come.

Again, he sent forth other servants, saying, Tell them which are bidden, Behold, I have prepared my dinner: my oxen and my fatlings are killed, and all things are ready: Come unto the marriage.

But they made light of it, and went their ways, one to his farm, another to his merchandise:

And the remnant took his servants, and entreated them spitefully, and slew them.

But when the King heard thereof, he was wroth: and he sent forth his armies, and destroyed those murderers, and burned up their city.

Thus saith he to his servants, The wedding is ready, but they which were bidden were not worthy.

Go ye therefore into the highways, and as many as ye shall find, bid to the marriage.

So those servants went out into the highways, and gathered together all as many as they found, both bad and good: and the wedding was furnished with guests.

And when the King came in to see the guests, he saw there a man which had not on a wedding garment:

And he saith unto him, Friend, how comest thou in hither not having a wedding garment? And he was speechless.

Then said the King to the servants, Bind him hand and foot, and take him away, and cast him into outer darkness; there shall be weeping and gnashing of teeth.

For many are called, but few are chosen wherefore all do not have on the wedding garment." (Matthew 22:2–14 JST)

This parable provides an invitation, a warning, and a promise that tie in with the Savior's concluding statement of the Sermon on the Mount.

God the Father invited the tribe of Judah and those other tribes who were in Palestine to return to him through Christ. Christ foretold that with Israel's refusal and the murder of God's servants, Jerusalem and Judah would be destroyed. Prior to the Second Coming of the Savior or the wedding feast, others would be bidden to attend. The Restoration of the gospel in the latter days is extending that invitation to attend the wedding feast to all of God's children (see Doctrine and Covenants 58:6–11; 65:3). In the parable, those who accepted the invitation were given attire appropriate to the occasion. At last, when the king arrived, a man was found without a wedding garment. This man was bound and thrown out because he hadn't entered as outlined by the king. To enter God's presence, one must be dressed in a wedding garment or have followed the steps God has required. Those who do not will not be allowed in God's presence. As the Savior taught, to enter God's kingdom we must listen and obey his teachings.

Thus, the Sermon on the Mount is completed. Christ has taught the leaders of his Church how they must live to be his disciples. They were also given instructions as to what to teach others who would follow Christ. The objective of all was to help those of God's children who desired to attend the wedding feast be garbed in the wedding garment.

ABOUT THE AUTHOR

E Wayne Stucki lives in St. George, Utah, with his wife, Franece. They have been married for forty-five years. Together they have five children and fifteen grandchildren. Wayne has a number of hobbies. He enjoys playing basketball, hiking, and camping in the nearby mountains or boating at Lake Powell. He reads all kinds of genres, including mystery, military, science fiction, and fantasy. What he enjoys most is spending time with his family.

www.ingramcontent.com/pod-product-compliance
Lightning Source LLC
LaVergne TN
LVHW041659070526
838199LV00045B/1125